THE COLOUR OF RESISTANCE

From the library of

THE COLOUR OF RESISTANCE
A Contemporary Collection of Writing by Aboriginal Women

ANTHOLOGIZED BY CONNIE FIFE

Sister Vision
Black Women and Women of Colour Press

ISBN 0-920813-62-3
1993 © copyright Connie Fife
Individual selections © copyright by their respective author(s)
1994 Second Printing

94 95 96 97 98 ML 098765432

The anthologizer wishes to thank CUSO for its financial support during the collection of these writings.

Canadian Cataloguing in Publication Data
Main entry under title:
Colour of Resistance

ISBN 0-920813-62-3

1. Canadian literature (English) - Indian authors.*
2. Canadian literature (English) - Women authors.*
3. Canadian literature (English) - 20th century.
4. Indians of North America - Canada - Women - Literary collections.
5. Women - Canada - Literary collections.
I. Fife, Connie, 1961-

PS8235.I5C65 1993   C810.8'0897   C93-094271-X
PR9184.5.I5C65 1993

Cover Painting: copyright © *Jaune Quick-to-See Smith*
Cover Design: *Stephanie Martin*
Book Layout and Design: *Hazelle Palmer*
Production: *Leela Achayra*
Editor for the Press: *Makeda Silvera*
Copy Editor: *Martha Sharpe*
Printed and Bound in Canada by Union Labour

Published by: **Sister Vision Press**
P.O. Box 217, Station E
Toronto, Ontario
Canada M6H 4E2

The publisher wishes to acknowledge the kind assistance of the Canada Council and the Ontario Arts Council towards its publishing program

Meegwetch to the Grandmothers who accompanied me on this journey and who stay with me no matter how short my footsteps. This collection of our various voices is for them, for they are the true colour of resistance.

FOREWORD

Five hundred years have passed since European contact, and in its wake a new form of resistance has emerged. While Native tradition has always been oral, and remains very much so, we have found a new means of responding to neo-colonialist literature.

The act of literary creation and our oral past have merged into a medium through which we can pass on not only the truth of our history but the moment in which we now exist. Our past, the present and the future come together through words that are "living" from their first conception to the time when the reader finds her own meaning in them. Within the pages of this anthology are words that carry their own life, having been birthed through the voices of Indigenous women who have chosen to re-invent how we resist, how we refuse to be silenced, and how we use contemporary tools to express old beliefs in order to lay the seeds for future generations.

At the turn of the century, E. Pauline Johnson must have understood that one day there would be other Native women like us who would also expand the borders of European literature based on our experiences, through our own eyes and in our own voices. There is no longer one literary standard by which to judge the written word, and each writer in this collection has re-defined the term "literature" by speaking in her own Indigenous voice, using her own style, and refusing to censor her own truth. *The Colour of Resistance* is a testament to our lives, a re-invention of our survival. In this book, Native women proclaim that "settler" literature is no longer acceptable as representative of our own creative process, nor does its confines do justice to our journey through the history of colonialism in our homeland.

CONTENTS

FICTION   133

ARTICLES & NON-FICTION   225

Introduction

THE INDIGENOUS RHYTHM AND TONE INVOKED IN THIS collection reflect our philosophy and world-view: Beginning with the internal, then journeying to the outer world, our creative selves remain central. We understand as women that to begin with the external means losing the moment of creation itself. While the writing in this anthology re-affirms the Native creative process, it also contains the distinct voices of women who have laboured with great love and courage through their internal journeys so that their truths are born whole and full of life in these pages. Despite all attempts at rendering these voices invisible in literature, they emerge clearly here, and louder than ever before.

Europe introduced us to the written word, to its devastating power when abused, and we Natives of North America became part of a long trail of genocide. Today the horror of the written word through the eyes of Christianity is reflected in the body of the land itself; her response is no longer subtle. Our response to such destruction — both culturally and environmentally — is found in much of our work.

Whether oral or visual, Indigenous literature has always existed throughout the Americas. Our collective memory remains intact regardless of any attempt to separate us from its origins. No matter the authors or their skills in the written word, European writers have failed miserably at conveying the essence behind our words; they have failed to transport the life we find in language onto the page. This is our struggle as Native writers, as women who inherently know the nature of birth: to bring to life a language that is at times lifeless. We struggle to transcend English in the sense that it has been overused and misunderstood by those who first brought it to us.

Language and memory; both are alive for us, both are essential to our individual well-being and that of our communities. We have found that the written word brought to our shores can and must be transformed into the sacred. Pivotal to our survival is the passing on of words from one generation to the next so that memory is not lost. Our stories should not be considered "traditional," for we understand it is not our place to decide that they belong in the public realm. But they are a re-invention of our capacity to survive.

The Native women writers in this anthology have given our sacred language new meaning. They have transformed a medium once used to oppress and silence us so that we might dwindle away without resistance. We have found that the written word does not have to be wrapped in the thoughts of the colonizer, but rather can convey the resilience of our survival. As Carolyn Dunn says:

So in the dying I live ...in the wasteland the hazards of my life begin anew. I have died a thousand times

not to be reborn but to live. And I survive. I tell the
stories of us, so that we can learn ..."

The Colour of Resistance has been a personal journey
for me, one that will remain with me for a long time. I am
grateful to each writer, each sister who sent in material
and offered words of encouragement and hope. Each and
every one of you made this collection possible; you are
why *The Colour of Resistance* was born. Walk in beauty.

Connie Fife
August 1993

Poetry

You too could have a fake Indian in your parlour
who'll never talk back
Fly in the face of it I want a plastic white man
I can blow up again & again
I want turkeys to keep their feathers
& the non-feathered variety to shut up
I want to bury these Indians dressed like cartoons of
our long dead
I want
to live
somewhere
where nobody is sold

CAROLYN DUNN

ancestors

lift your wing
letting stardust breezes
of rain
and tiny embers
of breath crystallize
I breathe water
to form from clay
my child's eyes
glow back at me
the mysteries of a
thousand-year-old starlight
in a flash of
dark
daylight
and star-driven
sky

JEANNETTE ARMSTRONG

Death Mummur

Yesterday I walked
by Thunderbird Park.
Tonight
With blood stained fingers,
I remove my mask,
I think
walk
past garish totem-painted store fronts,
down avenues that echo.

There are no Indians here.
None
even in the million dollar museum
that so carefully preserves
their clothing, their cooking utensils
their food;
for taxpayers
from all over
to rush their children by.

There are some Indians
hanging around Kings hotel
and they are dead,
preserved in alcohol.
It would be neater though

to kill us all at once.
Whole clans and tribes
could be dressed and stuffed.
Add a fifth floor to the museum
to accommodate us.
Better yet
pile us up like cordwood
in those longhouses
we would be home at last
and it would be good value.

I walk slowly and think back
I stagger under
the raw
hide pack
that I carry,
and the clever mask that I have fashioned
for myself,
from the bones and skin
of my dead tribe
and dipped in the fresh blood
of my brothers and sisters
scooped from old battle streets
near hotels.

JEANNETTE ARMSTRONG

First People

In the pre-dawn
moonset sprinkles silver dust
Out of water gleams
the voice of the loon rises
to cool mountains
Shivers the camp awake

A soft feeling
reaches outward
becomes sound
bursts into the still morning
like petals
opening shining surface
to the sun
The voice touches aware
the living

I bring the fire awake
Power
cupped in stone
flashes
touches wood
kindles warmth
and light is here

Whispering hush
itself a prayer
lifegiving water
smooths cool
over the body
washing the night shadows
swirls wake to sound
A clean rhythm
to touch the mind

Smooth and taut
coil upon coil
twining
life to life
winter to winter
time
encircles the first people
Weaves a dance
tracing tenuous patterns
in arranged layers
over all

Across the mind
wordless awareness
spreads in ripples
outward
tongues shape to feeling
voice and drum mesh
in a soft web

the magic of changers,
of the water beetle's part in creation
and
how two legged people came to be
moving us to ecstasies
our eyes almost in pain with wideness
at her tones,
matching hand stroked etching of
mountains
water fallings
running creatures
anything Grandmother wanted to show,
she didn't need the english
on which she had such a fragile hold,
it was the drama of her time
that filled our needs,
katydid keeps the tongue cherokee
hears our tales of then and now,
my memory hears Grandmother's
"aaay"
and smiles.

VICKIE SEARS

Oldways Keeper

Katydid
keeper of the
tongue of old
has stone stories saved
silently sung
sage songs
done
too seldom
by too few,
katydid clatters the night
reminding us of
who we are.
katydid knows how to
give it back
saves for sunshine
rides oconoluftee river
from hill to gulf
looking for
those who can listen,
cush cush le toong
ripples the windtaken katydid song
keep the ways

old as
now
then
tomorrow,
katydid knows the gift of the
selfsavoured smiles she sings
of Old Ones who
remember
and young ones who seek
all our relations.

CONNIE FIFE

Resistance

resistance is a woman
whose land is all on fire
perseverance and determination
are her daughters
she is a palestinian mother who
hands her children a legacy of
war together with the
weapons to fight in it
she is a black woman draped
in purple satin who strolls
down a runway allowing only
the clothes she wears to be sold
resistance is the absent native woman
who died at the hands of
a white artist
who lives inside herself
while thriving inside of me
resistance is a girl child who
witnesses her mother's death and
swears to survive no matter
where the hiding place
she is a woman beaten with hate
by the man she loves who
decides to escape to a world
where touch is sacred

resistance is the woman who defies
the male definition of love
and loves another woman
then heals an entire nation in doing so
she is a woman torn apart by
the barbed wire surrounding her home
who plots a way out
despite the consequences
resistance is every woman who
has ever considered taking up
arms writing a story leaving the abuse
saving her children or saving herself
she is every woman who dares
to stage a revolution complete a novel
be loved or change the world
resistance walks across a landscape
of fire accompanied by her daughters
perseverance and determination

CONNIE FIFE

Stones Memory

translucent stone murmured of my beginnings
whispered the secrets of my origins
called me home following nights of darkness
cried out for my return to sunlight
urged me to bring memory forward
compelled my circle to become complete
    round curve of mountains face
    showed herself to me in a blanket
    of blue and green expression
stories passed from palm to palm
trickled down my throat
etched their essence upon my heart
embedded their words within my ribcage
settled amongst my blood
    i remember her face
    recall her tone
    i remember my relatives
    their journey from water to land
i am reminded of every stone
who has ever spoken
ever wailed
ever celebrated
every stone whose birth
is evidence of creation
whose death harbours

I never moved in ways that might be interpreted as
loose. Instead, I became what Jean Rhys phrased,
"aggressively respectable." I'd be so goddamned
respectable that white people would feel slovenly in
my presence.

newo

> squaw is to whore
> as
> Indian maiden is to virgin
>
> squaw is to whore
> as
> Indian princess is to lady

niyanan

I would become the Indian princess not the squaw
dragging her soul after laundry, meals, needy kids,
and abusive husbands. These were my choices. I could
react naturally, spontaneously to my puberty, my
newly discovered sexuality or I could be mindful of the
squaw whose presence hounded my every choice.

nikotwasik

squawman:

a man who is seen with lives with laughs with
a squaw.

"squawman"

a man is a man is a whiteman   until

he is a squaw he is a squaw he is a squawman

MARILYN DUMONT

Memories of a really good brown girl

you are not good enough, not good enough, obviously not
good enough, the chorus is never loud or conspicuous, just
there

carefully dressed, hair combed like I am going to the
doctor, I follow my older sister, we take the short-cut
by the creek, through the poplar and cottonwood trees,
along sidewalks, past the pool hall, hotel, variety store,
the United Church, over the bridge, along streets until
we reach the school pavement, it is at this point that I
sense my sister's uneasiness, no obvious signs, just her
silence, she is holding my hand like she holds her
breath, she has changed subtly since we left home. We
enter a set of doors which resemble more a piece of
machinery than a doorway, with metal handles, long
glass windows, and iron grates on the floor, the halls
are long and white, our feet echo as we walk. I feel as
though I've been wrapped in a box, a shoe box where
the walls are long and manilla gloss, it smells of paper
and glue, there are shuffling noises I've never heard
before and kids in the rooms we pass by. We enter a
room from what seems the back door, rows of small
tables lined up like variety cereal boxes, other small
faces look back vacant and scared next to the teacher's
swelling smile. (I have learned that when whites smile

that fathomless smile, it's best to be wary.) I am handed over to the teacher, later I would reflect upon this simple exchange between my older sister and the teacher as the changing of the guard, of big sister to teacher, and before that when I was even younger, of mother to big sister.

This is my first day of school and I stand alone; I look on. Most of the kids know what to do, like they've been here before, like the teacher is a friend of the family. I am a foreigner, I stay in my seat, frozen, afraid to move, afraid to make a mistake, afraid to speak, they talk differently than I do, I don't sound the way they do, but I don't know how to sound any different, so I don't talk, don't volunteer answers to questions the teacher asks, I become invisible.

I don't glisten with presence, confidence, glisten with the holiness of St. Anne whose statue I see every year at the pilgrimage, her skin translucent, like the holy ghost is a light and it shines out through her fluorescent skin, as if a sinless life makes your skin a receptacle of light. The other kids have porcelain skin like St. Anne, too, but unlike her, they have little blond hairs growing out of small freckles on their arms, like the kind of freckles that are perfectly placed on the noses of the dolls I got each Christmas, in fact, the girls in my class look like my dolls, bumpy curls, geometric faces, crepe paper dresses, white legs and patent shoes.

My knees are scarred, have dirt ground in them from crawling under fences, climbing trees, riding skid horses, and jumping from sawdust piles. I remember, once when I was a flower girl for my brother's wedding, I was taken home to the city by my brother's white fiancee and she "scrubbed the hell out of me." All other events that took place on that visit are diminished by the bathtub staging, no other event was given as much time and attention by her. I was fed and watered like a lamb for slaughter. I was lathered, scrubbed, shampooed, exfoliated, medicated, pedicured, manicured, rubbed down, and moisturized. When it was over, I felt that every part of my body had been hounded of dirt and sin and that now I, like St. Anne, had become a receptacle of light.

My skin always gave me away. In grade one, I had started to forget where I was when a group of us stood around the sink at the back of the class washing up after painting and a little white girl stared at the colour of my arms, and exclaimed, "Are you ever brown!" I wanted to pull my short sleeves down to my wrists and pretend that I hadn't heard her, but she persisted, "Are you Indian?" I wondered why she had chosen this ripe time to ask me and if this was the first she'd noticed?

How could I respond? If I said yes, she'd reject me,

worse, she might tell the other kids my secret and then they'd laugh and shun me. If I said no, I'd be lying, and when they found out I was lying, they'd shun me.

I said "No" and walked away.

I just watched and followed, I was good at that, good at watching and following. It was what I did best, and I learned quickly by watching. (Some learning theories say that native kids learn best by watching, because they're more visual. I always knew that I learned by watching to survive in two worlds and in a white classroom.) I only needed to be shown something once and I remembered it, I remembered it in my fibre.

I lived a dual life, I had white friends and I had Indian friends and the two never mixed and that was normal. I lived on a street with white kids, so they were my friends after school. During school I played with the Indian kids. These were kids from the other Indian families who were close friends with my parents. At school, my Indian friends and I would play and function quite comfortably in our own group, like the white kids did in theirs.

I am looking at a school picture, grade five, I am smiling easily. My hair is shoulder length, curled, a page-boy, I am wearing a royal blue dress. I look poised, settled like I belong. I won an award that year for most improved student. I learned to follow really well.

I am in a university classroom, an english professor corrects my spoken english in front of the class. I say "really good," he says, "You mean, really well, don't you?" I glare at him and say emphatically, "No, I mean really good."

KIMBERLY BLAESER

Sewing Memories: This Poem I've Wanted to Write

I.

You know there's this poem I've wanted to write
    about sewing
    And it has stories in it
    like about the time
    I sewed the sleeves in my dress upside-down
    so the elbow darts lay across the vein on my inner
arm
Or about the time you applied for that job
    at the sewing factory
    and came home embarassed and laughing at
    yourself
    because you kept answering all the questions on
    the application
    the same way
    saying how you love to sew
Or about the time you sewed the prom dress for me
    and followed a store-bought pattern
    only to discover that I wasn't exactly made
    like the model for that pattern
    I still remember the shock we had
    when I tried on that dress
    and the upper half of my breasts

along with the buttons and rickrack and scribbled
notes
that had collected there through the years
I remember losing track of time as I studied the crazy
quilt
in one of the bedrooms in the old part of the house
trying to find pieces of fabric I could match
with whole things that had been made from the
same cloth
And I rather think I'm doing the same thing now

So finally today I think to myself about
how you used to make your own patterns
drawing them carefully, cutting them out of
newspaper
How we used to plot to find ways to use flawed
material
that we could get on sale
Or looked expectantly through dimestore bundles
always finding that one not-too-ugly for imagining
roll of cloth that became curtains or pyjamas
I remember the patched corner of the first quilt I ever
made
the yellow and print squares all perfect
but for that single one
the corner I folded under
whenever I wrapped my cry-baby doll
I still like to see her all cozy where she lies
among the other dusty treasures

Do you remember
> how Debbie's grandmother used to think I had
> strange ideas about sewing
> like the time I ran the stripes in the yoke of a top
> vertically
> while in the rest of the top I ran them horizontally

Or the times I made that flocked drindle skirt
> that red white and blue fuzzy pillow

Into all those things we made
> we sewed bits of our bodies
> and bits of our dreams
> we stitched in errors more bold
> than those required in sand paintings

And what we created seemed truly to be ours
> because we did them that way
> filled with make-believe and mistakes
> instead of the usual way
> and maybe this poem about sewing
> refused to come out for such a long time
> because I was trying to follow someone else's
> perfect pattern

So I thought I'd just make it our way
> lay the memories and stories out
> zig-zag through time
> and stitch them together the way I see them

and thus care less and less each year
that what we have constructed or sown with our
lives
may not be perfect
for the blemishes and errors
we tried to hide in the corners
make that love more dear
for not having given at the seams

All of these things I feel in that one air burst of
memory
    that comes as I unfold the stories
    shake off the dust
    hold them out in front of me
    or gaze at them across my body in a full-length
    mirror
    I feel their age upon me and count their years
    and yet I know too
    how young these stories are
    and how they will live
    whether or not I save
    the pieces of cloth
    into which we sewed the stories
Suddenly I feel my own insignificance
    and hurry to put them gently back
    so as not to disturb too much
    the power they have accumulated

One of the best things about the threads in this sewing

is that they keep pulling in more
more people, more years, more colours of events
and the stitches can attach all the things of
memory
not just flat and smooth pieces of cloth
but bits of fur added for design
a fringe at the bottom instead of a hem
ribbons of all colours and fabrics
even the jingles like on the dance dresses
the smell of pine sap that never really washes
away
but sinks into fabrics
and lingers forever like the sweetgrass smell of
baskets
the taste and heaviness of leather
the swish of corduroy rubbing together on my legs
the filmy seduction of sheers and lace
the colours and patterns of beads
all things sewn together
so much like memories
stitched sometimes in hidden seams
sometimes boldly patched together
with unmatched fabrics and unmatched threads
knowing that sometimes usefulness
counts more than beauty
And when I see the tiny patchworks
hung in country galleries
captioned and bartered for
I know we have this masterpiece

KIMBERLY BLAESER

Living History

Walked into Pinehurst, sunburned, smelling of fish,
Big Indian man paying for some gas and a six pack,
Looking at me hard.
Dreamer, I think. Too old for me.
Heads right toward me.
"Jeez," he says, "You look just like your mom —
You must be Marlene's girl."
Pinches my arm, but I guess it's yours
he touches.
Hell, wasn't even looking at me.
Wonder if I'm what they call living history?

KIMBERLY BLAESER

Certificate of Live Birth: Escape from the Third Dimension

"We do indeed have four dimensions. But even in relativity, they are not all of the same sort. Only three are spatial. The fourth is temporal; and we are unable to move freely in time. We cannot return to days gone by, nor avoid the coming of tomorrow. We can neither hasten nor retard our journey into the future."*

I.

Shuffling papers
    rushing to find some critical
    form or letter or journal
    mired amid the stacks that have collected
    that I've hidden in every corner of the room

Tiny new-born footprints step out of flatland
    a xerox copy of my birth certificate
Nostalgia
    no time —
Yet as I hold the single sheet
    it shapes itself and curves out of my hand

Chubby ankle circled firmly
    protesting kicking held still

foot inked
the page indelibly marked
   with my unwilling signature
Perhaps some memory of that first helplessness
   makes me struggle still against capture
   against hint of bonds —
You won't imprint me again

———

"Our fourth dimension, time, true dimension though it
be, does not permit us to escape from a three-
dimensional prison. It does enable us to get out, for if
we wait patiently for time to pass, our sentence will be
served and we shall be set free. That is hardly an
escape, however. To escape we must travel through
time to some moment when the prison is wide open, or
in ruins, or not yet built; and then, having stepped
outside, we must reverse the direction of our time
travel to return to the present."*

II.

Or perhaps it was your capture
   that so enraged my yet unconscious mind
   that brought me kicking into the world

For yours was the more torturous:
> Father, caucasian.
> Mother, caucasian.

What pain what shame what fear
> must have forced that check in that flatland box?

Mother, should I correct it?

But no it is more accurate
> just as it stands

In that mark I read your life
I read the history of Indian people in this country
It is my heritage more truly than any account of
bloodlines
It tells the story of a people's capture
It tells the story of a people's struggle to survive

And, Mother, this poem is the certificate of our live
birth
For together we have escaped their capture
Our time together out distances their prison
It "stands in ruins" within the circle of our lives:
> Father, caucasian.
> Mother, American Indian
> Daughter, mixed blood.

*Quotations taken from Banesh Hoffman's introduction to *Flatland: A Romance of Many Dimensions* by Edwin A. Abbott.

GAIL TREMBLAY

Reveal His Name

A voyage charted by stars
bears crosses to an island,
bears blood, severs hands
that shaped ceremonies to nurture
Earth, stains,
              stains,
                    stains,
stains the holy dirt, opens
continents to rape;

don't call him explorer ——
(—— Butcher is his hidden name)
reveal his hidden name ——
reveal his name.

ROBERTA HILL WHITEMAN

Breaking Trail

Here basswood leaves soak up
evening sun, their phosphorescent leaves
glistening like scum on the surface
of the pond we passed just now.

Our children are leaving, taking
the rue and the red light of sunrise
with them. Soon the wind will pile
their clothes in the southwest corner

of the sky. We followed trails our parents
took, and others. We cut our own brush
oftentime. We pushed through mud so deep,
our children knew its danger and detoured.

Yet on days like this in midsummer,
singing fills my soul when
under the ecstasy of leaves
we find the way worms work leaves

into lace and wing. Stepping over a log,
you hold out your hand behind you.
I grasp your warm fingers
and once again, we trudge in sunlight,

Filling myself with sound, I answer,
dew sparkling on grass and green
around me. Drifting through my daily life,
I'm blanketed by this memory bordering on dream.
The ruby hum of that conversation
makes me listen when earth awakens
her green beings, and they begin to speak
our first language of motion and colour
and connection. One of the dispossessed,
I took from the sunflower a talisman,
a seed kept in the cave of my soul, to remind me
both silence and song belong to the earth.

KATERI DAMM

Grandmother, Grandfather

i carry a picture of you
in my head
i carry your blood in my heart
i carry a cross
since you went away

i lost your words
i lost the sound of your voice

my skin is made of spirits
at night i feel them dance
my hair is a thousand feathered arrows
my face a dull moon

i carry a picture of you in my head

KATERI DAMM

Why This Woman
(For Jo-anna and Pietra Anna)

why this earth
in solemn patterns
turns
why this sun
circles nightly
casting shadows across the sinking front porch
swing
why this woman
in holy wonder
repeats the human story
why this child
grows in beauty
laughs and cries
lives
turning never escaping
this simple narrative spins us
into reflections
versions of each other

turning turning
we watch
as brightly shines the moon

KATERI DAMM

To You Who Would Wage War Against Me

I.

there are many lines
you have not traced on my palms
still
you think you know me

when i speak
you nod knowingly
as if
you've already read my mind
and are only politely acknowledging
the confirmation of my spoken words

II.

but you cannot possibly know
what i've been contemplating
these days

my head is full of blood
but you show no fear
and i do not trust my hands
which feel to me like stones

you do not cower when i approach
though i am like a runaway train
and i can hear your voice
cool and steady
while my brain screams profanities
into the air around your ears

our past has given you no reason
to be afraid
but still i am surprised you cannot see
the danger burning brightly in my eyes
the fire i am struggling to control

III.

as i sit stewing in the kitchen's false
light
with tears my daughter
comes to me
frightened by what she cannot see
afraid tonight to sleep

i hold her in my arms
singing soft words of comfort
feeling her heart quickly
beating against my chest
knowing before i can think
that i have forgotten us
for our stupid little war

knowing in the incandescent light
that anger will never move me
as delicately as she has moved me this
night

Nicole Tanguay

Ogokwe

Two Spirited Woman
stripped to the core
she undresses to expose
the softness of her fruit
blood red glistening to the world
singing here I am
come close come touch
the fire that has burned
for thousands of years come
see her fruit swell
and give life over and
over and over always
remaining blood red
glistening to the world
two spirited woman
Ogokwe

NICOLE TANGUAY

Where Will the Children Play

They have raped and tortured your body
taken your soul and sold it for more greed

Postcards from long ago will show our grandchildren
what an evergreen tree looked like
concrete jungles will be the playing ground
children will have to play on

I have seen death and destruction first hand as I
walked thru what used to be a forest
of living creatures
now as you look there is nothing but a sense of
loneliness
nothing remains except the reality of
what the future will bring

In seven generations what will be left
sky that is made from the deserts
that used to be rainforests
houses with no windows to see the
effects of their forefathers

And you sit there in your fancy restaurants
discussing the colour of your favourite lipstick
how many stocks to buy

which nation to invade today

And my brothers and my sisters worry
about the lack of food and the fear
of no warm clothes for their young

And you tell me you are happy

NICOLE TANGUAY

Half Breed

2 sets of arms
    reach across
2 different cultures
    to give birth to
2 different entities
    in one

Half breed = Half Devil
    Metis Mestiza Hupa
    Combo

2 in one equals
    discrimination amongst
2 different cultures

I fight I struggle to keep
    identities
I fight I struggle to keep
    2 feet planted
    in one
    self

KIM CALDWELL

Bad Taste in My Mouth

today resentment fills me
    turning my stomach
leaving a bad taste in my mouth

you first question my "authenticity"
    then you bombard me with rude questions
that you call interest in my people
    and the saddest part to me
is that you don't even know
    you are being disrespectful

no, I don't know what the symbol
    on your genuine Navajo necklace means
I am not Navajo
    and your distant Indian relatives
long buried and remembered only when
    you see an Indian you can tell about them
don't mean I will tell you all about me
    and call you relative.

and what would you say if I even
    mentioned your disrespect
and asked you to just
    let me be.

and what would you do if I told you
    that having "cultural understanding"
really means to just
    let me be.

because today my heart is fatigued
    and the fatigue comes from
being expected to teach you
    about myself
when there are no words to tell you
    without meeting your resistance and
your self righteous disbelief
    being directed at me —
and then at the next native person you meet.

my life is not on display
    for your museum-goer curiosity
my beliefs are not yours
    to dissect and disseminate.

hell, half the time I'm not even
    sure who I am
and yet the expectation is that
    you will somehow listen
as you wait impatiently
for me to prove who

    all native people are ...
in a half hour lunch conversation

or waiting for a bus
you want it all

condensed
correlated
and made easy to digest.

today resentment fills me
turning my stomach
leaving a bad taste in my mouth.

LENORE KEESHIG-TOBIAS

He Fights
(bear iv)

They have been
talking, those ones,
talking, saying as
he grows older,
he becomes graceful
in his lumbering,
he becomes more
bear-like

secretly, he dreams
of bear, and
struggles hard
to let go of it, let
go of things
that hold Indian people
back, things that
pull them back,
back into
the white
man's dark ages

and he well knows
the importance
of becoming a
man, modern in wanting

progress and other
white man things

openly, he fights
his children
those searching,
those trailing,
tracking and bumbling,
and yet, as the years
wear on, he walks
more and more
like the bear
they seek

LENORE KEESHIG-TOBIAS

Eagle Dance

You are
watching
some kind of
movement
— a dance

Figurants turn
toward you and
thrust over your
head a mask

Muslin
shrouds your vision
until your eyes
can measure distance
through the dark threads

Your fingers grasp
the wing tips

Arms spread
poised
your feet begin
the light double-steps
making circles wide

and tranquil
over the floor

Another figurant
approaches
quickly to loosen
your fingers' grasp
and let you know
there is no need
to hold so tight
— your fingers
can soar

Your fingers
feather
time and space

Someone's fishing
tackle threatens to
embed a fish hook
deep into your calf

You compress your
circle
calmly and
continue serenely
the Eagle's dance.

LENORE KEESHIG-TOBIAS

O Canada
(bear v)

O Canada — your provinces shout
O Canada — your country shouts
O Canada — your people shout
Our home and native land

(Our home, your settled land)

Closed your eyes and righteous words
have never made us disappear,
nor protected you from the bad dream,
your reality, your history, your lie

Listen. Your provinces, your cities
shout out our names — Quebec,
Ontario, Manitoba, Saskatchewan ...
Toronto, Winnipeg, Saskatoon, Ottawa

Your country too, eh, O Ken-a-tah

We have always walked on the edge
of your dreams, stalked
you as you made wild your way

through this great land,
generation after generation
And, O Canada, you have always been
Afraid of us, scared, because you know
you can never live without us

Nancy Cooper

The Watchmen

I went to the heart of the steel and glass today.
To visit with the watchmen
Who should be

Watching

Eagles fly

Whales play

Salmon flash

Instead their reflection shines off an escalator.

For ten thousand years they have watched over land
That is so green
So vast
So beautiful.
Well I guess the concrete stretches as far now
And furniture stores can be beautiful.

No eagles cry

And clamshells don't litter the sidewalk.

Nancy Cooper

Raven Comes Aboard

You speak the tales of your people
And the Raven comes alive
To tantalize, trick and awaken
Awaken within me the history
Knowledge of a time other than this here and now.
The trickster survives and dwells
In eastern woodland lodges
And over there in your Haida soul.
I in my clamshell preaching my Indianness to the air.
No, you caw caw and sputter
There is nothing called non-status
Never half of anything
Only all of you.
You speak the tales of your people
And Raven comes alive
And Raven comes calling
Meegwetch
Howa
Voice of ten thousand lives ago.

NANCY COOPER

Untitled

Ok.
So I'm not princess Pocahontas
And I didn't even want to be
Indian
Native
Wagonburner
First Nation
Aboriginal
Squaw
For 18 years.
Where does that leave me?
And who is carrying around the
"Indianness" ruler,
Measurement of tradition
3/4 cup of Anishnawbe kwe?
But.
I can say hello — ANIIN
I love my mother
And the other one
Mother of us all.
I burn the sage and my
Soul opens further each day
To let in the years
Years
Years

Years
I lost.
I've stood on the shores of oceans
And turned my
Back on the mountains
Throwing all the "whys"
To the tides.
They came back.
I can wait for the full moon.
I can wait.
For answers that will have been with me
Forever.
Just forgotten
Just hidden.

Linda Hogan

It Must Be

I am an old woman
whose skin looks young
though I ache
and have heard the gravediggers call me
by name.

The pathologists come
with their forceps and gowns.
It must be a disease, they say.
it must be.

It must be, they say
over there in the joints
that her grandmother refuses to bend
one more time
though her face smiles at the administrators
taking reports.

The doctors come
with their white coats and masks.
It must be
her heart, let us cut her open with knives.

Doctor, did you hear the singing in my heart?
Or find the broken-off love, the lost brother?

You must have witnessed all the old women
who live in the young house of this body
and how they are full of black wool
and clipped nails.
They know what must be.

They make me carry on
under my jeans and sweater,
traditions and complaints about the sad
state of the nation.

They have big teeth
for biting through leather and birch bark
and lies
about the world
They have garlic in their pockets
to protect us from the government.

The nurses arrive with pink nails
and the odour of smoke. They arrive
from lifting the hips of old men
as if they were not old men.

One of the old women inside
lashes out at the nurses
and all who remain girls,
and at the bankers and scholars.
But despite that old woman,

there are days I see my girlish hands
and wonder which banker owns them
and there are nights I watch the wrong face
in the mirror, and afternoons
I hold that face down to the floor by its neck
with those banker's hands,
those scholar's hands
that wish to silence the old woman inside
who tells the truth
and how it must be.

And there are days
the old women gossip and sing,
offering gifts of red cloth and cornbread
to one another
On those days I love the ancestors
in and around me,
the mothers of trees and deer
and harvests, and that crazy one
in her nightgown
barring herself to the world,
daring the psychiatrists to come
with their couches and theories and rats.
On those days the oldest one is there,
taking stock
in all her shining
and with open hands.

Joy Harjo

*For Anna Mae Pictou Aquash, Whose Spirit Is Present Here and in the
Dappled Stars (for we remember the story and must tell it again so we
may all live)*

Beneath a sky blurred with mist and wind,
                  I am amazed as I watch the violet
heads of crocuses erupt from the stiff earth
                after dying for a season,
as I have watched my own dark head
                appear each morning after entering
the next world
      to come back to this one,
                amazed.
It is the way in the natural world to understand the
place
                the ghost dancers named
after the heart/breaking destruction.
              Anna Mae,
                everything and nothing changes.
You are the shimmering young woman
              who found her voice,
when you were warned to be silent, or have your body
cut away
from you like an elegant weed.
    You are the one whose spirit is present in the
dappled stars.

(They prance and lope like coloured horses who stay
with us
through the streets of these steely cities. And I have
seen them
    nuzzling the frozen bodies of tattered drunks
                          on the corner.)

This morning when the last star is dimming
                and the buses grind toward
the middle of the city, I know it is ten years since they
buried you
    the second time in Lakota, a language that could
                      free you.
I heard about it in Oklahoma, or New Mexico,
      how the wind howled and pulled everything
down
in a righteous anger.
      (It was the women told me) and we
understood wordlessly
the ripe of meaning of your murder.

As I understand ten years later after the slow changing
                of the seasons
that we have just begun to touch
    the dazzling whirlwind of our anger,
we have just begun to perceive the amazed world the
ghost dancers
    entered
        crazily, beautifully.

In February 1976, the unidentified body of a young woman was found on the Pine Ridge Reservation in South Dakota. The official autopsy attributed death to exposure. The FBI agent present at the autopsy ordered her hands severed and sent to Washington for fingerprinting. John Trudell rightly called this mutilation an act of war. Her unnamed body was buried. When Anna Mae Aquash, a young Micmac woman who was an active American Indian Movement member, was discovered missing by her friends and relatives, a second autopsy was demanded. It was then discovered she had been killed by a bullet fired at close range to the back of her head. Her killer or killers have yet to be identified.

Joy Harjo

The Real Revolution Is Love

I argue with Roberto on the slick-tiled patio
where houseplants as big as elms sway in a samba
breeze at four or five in the Managua morning
after too many Yerbabuenas and as many shots of
golden rum. And watch Pedro follow Diane up
her brown arm, over the shoulder of her cool dress,
the valleys of her neck to the place inside her
ear where he isn't speaking revolution. And Alonzo
tosses in the rhetoric made of too much rum and
the burden of being an American in a country
he no longer belongs to.

What we are dealing with here are ideological
differences, political power, he says to
impress a woman who is gorgeously intelligent
and who reminds me of the soft talc desert
of my lover's cheek. She doesn't believe
anything but the language of damp earth
beneath a banana tree at noon, and will soon
disappear in the screen of rum, with a man
who keeps his political secrets to himself
in favour of love.

I argue with Roberto, and laugh across the
continent to Diane, who is on the other side

of the flat, round table whose surface ships
would fall off if they sailed to the other
side. We are *Anishnabe* and *Creek. We have wars
of our own.* Knowing this we laugh and laugh,
until she disappears into the poinsettia forest
with Pedro, who is still arriving from Puerto Rico.

Palm trees flutter in smouldering tongues.
I can look through the houses, the wind, and hear
Jennifer's quick laughter become a train
that has no name. Columbus doesn't leave the
bow of the slippery ship, and Allen is standing at the
rim of Momotombo, looking into the blue, sad rain
of a boy's eyes. They will come back tomorrow.

*This is the land of revolution. You can do anything
you want,* Roberto tries to persuade me. I fight my way
through the cloud of rum and laughter,
through the lines of
Spanish and spirits of the recently dead whose elbows
rustle the palm leaves. It is almost dawn and we are
still a long way from morning, but never far enough
to get away.

I do what I want, and take my revolution to bed with
me, alone. And awake in a story told by my ancestors
when they spoke a version of the very beginning,
of how so long ago we climbed the backbone of these
tortuous Americas. I listen to the splash of the Atlantic

and Pacific and see Columbus land once more,
over and over again.

This is not a foreign country, but the land of our
dreams.

I listen to the gunfire we cannot hear, and begin
this journey with the light of knowing
the root of my own furious love.

BETH CUTHAND

The Anglais, They Say

In the voices of Louis Riel

The anglais they say
I am crazy
The francophone   and   the Metis.

But you   old man
Why   do you smile?

Because you are gifted Louis
with second sight like me

But you are not a man.
They   do not perceive
you   as such
You   are a savage
who drifts
      over crosses
and churches
      and votive candles.

Louis, learn to use this gift.
Smoke your pipe and wear your sash.

If I am gifted
    as you say
Why?
    do you   allow me
        to suffer?
Why?
    do you turn   into silent
    wings
    that disappear
    in the night?

LEE MARACLE

For Paula Gunn Allen

I know who shaman's daughter is
he lives in the body of a woman
— a moulting bird
a snake, cloaked in sloughing dress
an orchid unfolding.

I know who shaman's daughter is
she lives in the body of a man,
nurturing the pulchitrude
of butterflies metamorphosis
cherishing magic chaos,

I know who shaman's daughter is
turtle island's trickster,
full of herself. She plays out
our painful growth, she knows
courage resides in healing laughter

I know who shaman's daughter is
she lives the music of the earth's
orchestrated maturity,
her continuing transformation
but womanly blossoming.

The rhythm of her he-body
hears the music of change
the anguish of listening
spiralling down to the embarrassing
moment of discovery.

I know who shaman's daughter is
this manwoman who knows
the simplicity of
earth's revolution is worth
a joke or two

There is no place for her
Still,
the orchid of his intellect
teases new life from the confused
inner places of turtle island.

DORIS SEALE

On Getting Published

Knowing better,
They took our words,
so carefully set
down
in a certain way
one beside another —
    we were intent to say
    exactly what we meant —
And rearranged them
to fit
some concept of the mind
some alien bent
from another place and time.

We are at home
And not at home
Where even our words
May be used
Against us

Doris Seale

Well I Too Am Through With All That Stuff

When I think of all the women,
All the beautiful women
Who think they're
Stupid
Weak
Worthless
Because they're old
Fat
Indian
Disabled
Or some other throwaway thing
Hung on them by someone with nothing better to do
in life than pass judgement,
When I think of the children
Never to grow old,
And the Old Ones lived to see
Their children go
Before them,
And the men
Standing with empty hands,
Unlearned
Anything
Not coming out of a bottle,
When I think of their shame,
When I think of their goodness wasted,

It's not enough to say to *them*,
Those namers,
It's not enough to say
You're walking around dead, anyway,
I can smell you start to rot.
I want to hang them upside down
Over a hot little fire,
I want to take my knife and slowly
Cut a thousand pieces of their skin
Until their cold superiority runs out of them
Like red rivers.
I want to see knowledge grow behind their eyes,
See them understand
Just before they die,
What their god meant when he said
Suffer the little ones,
And I want it to take a long, long time.

COLLEEN FIELDER

Metis Woman

Metis woman alone and angry
still
Your genes seed no contentment
in the child yet unborn
Your taut nerves waiting
the fill of an empty cup
Priestess of the wild
challenging anywhere
the homeless ones
the curious the men
of all kinds
Seekers who leave
their mark on you
Better to run than face them
or stay becoming weaker

Restless journeys take you
many places
escaping a lot of ways
here and there
Metis woman alone
midst all the faces

No Indian nor other forebear
could understand your fear
or pride or pain
The way you drifted
waiting for the rain

COLLEEN FIELDER

Other Dreams

I crossed the earth in my sleeping
Faces watched from my ceiling
Moonlit lovers covered by wind
and branches
Shadows on their pillows
tangled old arbutus cedar
arms flailing
holding onto rocks and daisies
Your hands full of ocean
We lift our arms and wave them
dancing trees swaying
The wind in them
There are breezes with no trees
to sway in
No mountain bushes
to rustle through
Alone they are gentle as moss
to a falling leaf
Together they have other dreams

DEBRA HAALAND TOYA

I Am 1000 Years Old

My bones are strong as Shiprock

My heart is as soft as the sand fringing the San Jose

I take in the beliefs and fears that percolate
up from the dirt
and swirl about in the house of my grandmother

I look like the ancient ones

I hunt like the warriors

I teach children to believe in
clear, blue, sweet water, and sparrow hawk

My teeth are yet unbroken
as when I chewed sinew to make moccasins

My voice is as powerful as the Black Bear's
resonating through the granite canyon

I am the manifestation of all my people from time
immemorial
they will utter great words, write, and practise life
through me

And I will learn

Jeanetta Calhoun

Another Saturday Night . . .

1
a hawk hurled itself into a plate glass window
i took his wings and tail feathers
offered tobacco for his spirit

you were on an airplane flying east

2
on 42nd Street in New York City and 10th Street
in Oklahoma City and on a thousand other bitter
streets
your dark eyes gaze into the rancid air aching
with regrets and mourning for yesterdays

the bottle of thunderbird in your hand in irony
an anaesthesia
for the hungry belly and the screaming heart

3
in a clear star field in western Oklahoma
a tipi rises from a red dust whirlwind
the moon grows luminous in song
hawk feathers carry blessings across the
empty cup of america

listen
they are calling you home

Jeanetta Calhoun

Untitled
(For Hog's daughter*)

roses line the grey steel fence
the thorns draw blood from my fingers
and remind me i am alive

the petals are the only thing that sustains me
the only colour
the only softness within my grasp

all my tomorrows are spent
this second, this breath
are all that belong to me

**A woman warrior among the Cheyennes, one of the few to
survive the escape from Fort Robinson and the Last Hole fight.*

JEANETTA CALHOUN

Storyteller
(For Iness Little Sanderson)

i drive toward the arms of the arkansas river
it calls to me
jealous of the hudson murmuring beneath my window
through long winter nights

in oklahoma an owl waits silently
amid the rubble of my grandmother's house
her face shines out from its eyes
its wings brush the edges of my wandering solitude

rain sequins the windshield
a shy moon hides itself behind a veil of black clouds
radio stations fade with the passage of miles

grandmother
you were silenced before you could
finish telling me the stories
i am coming home
i am listening everywhere
for your voice

ANNHARTE

Blueberry Canoe

Flirty wind tugged at her blanket.
    he whispered "let's play."

She told him "Go away I fast for my vision."
    She tucked the blanket ends around her knees.
He pried out a diamond from a lone star on her back.
    He twirled and put it in a pine branch.
    He murmured "just like a puzzle."
    He took every shape she thought hers.
    He saved the bear paws for last.
    He gathered hatchets, arrows, and trails.
    Didn't know what was missing.
    He blew chilliness under her rib cage.
Her shoulders hunched but she knew he still hunted.

Her grand design had been Moon Over Tipi.

    she escaped her mother's scolding
    that day she put those blueberries in a canoe
    it was the biggest souvenir hanging on the tripod
    tourists laughed at her purple creation
    her mother lost a dollar sale

the mark in her memory when her mother left
a suitcase of shells, beads, and a moosehide vest
    strange toys for her kid's play
    instead she played secretary
she pushed old papers under the sewing machine
    presser foot up treadling her invoices
    bills of lading, cancelled cheques

"Stop it Windy" she said abruptly.
He got too close to the tipi in the back
of her mind with the moon held above.
Over his head, too, she amused herself
with Twotimer/Too much timely
Her moment.

Nevermind
He didn't spoil her history
He might undo her stitches
He didn't unravel her mind

Laura Tohe

Blue Horses Running

New possibilities exist with you
    where sagebrush dots the desertscape.
    where a string of crows float like black beads on a
    turquoise sky and where mountains hold plants spread
    out like a blanket

We travel the colours of brilliant red rock cliffs
    that form within ancestral space
    we travel on the colours of the rainbow
    and know what it means to come forth, to awaken

Here it's possible to know that you belong to the earth
    in a language that names us,
    that his place formed you,
    and craved the high bones in your face

Cedar and rock monoliths know the motion of wind.
    the patience of waiting, the gathering of strength
    here it's possible to know the world in the words of our
    ancestors the simplistic beauty of blue horses running

HAUNANI-KAY TRASK

Woman

where are you drawn
to: moon, mountains
long, hard beaches
at starless midnight

or does the sound
of thunder incite
and frighten you
to come closer

over the shallows
into the arms
of those astride
a sun-burnt sea

sharks and mantas
under the surface
dangerous
against the blue

waiting for you
your sullen blood
your silver eye
your fanged desire

to be raw
swift
and deadly

HAUNANI-KAY TRASK

Sisters

I.

doves in the rain
remind me of us
mornings above
Kane'ohe bay blue
sheen stillness
across long waters gliding
to coconut island

channels of sound
colour   rhythmic
currents   shell
picking   jellyfish
hunting   squeals
of mischief oblivious
in the calm

II.

rain pours
steady clouding
the light   dark
mornings darker
evenings silted

in the night   smell of dead
fish   dead
limu   dead
reef

eight million
for coconut island
five hundred thousand
for townhouses
on the hill   traffic
and greedy foreigners
by the mile

III.

destruction as a way
of life   clever
haole culture
killing as it goes

"no stone
left unturned"
no people
left untouched

IV.
in every native
place   a pair
of sisters
driven by the sound
of doves

the colour of
morning
defending life
with the spear
of memory

limu   seaweed
haole   foreigner, white people

Heid Ellen Erdrich

The Tree That's Gone
For a long ago Cheryl

Not even a stump left
where that fir stood —
where you ran dumb drunk,
your knot of grief unbound
though all week you had tied it
so tightly it set your mouth in a line,
narrowed your eyes to black curves,
yanked your head straight in its secret.
Drink cut it loose:
you stumbled, hollering to the air
in words so far from their tribe,
no one could translate —
wails that cracked the cold night,
made the stars split the sky.

Little Woman,
I'll never speak your words,
but I understand and understand
the sorrow you cried into that tree's roots.
It's gone now, died of your pain.
Your tears drained into the ground,
the tree tapped their hot waters,
drank so deeply it shook,

sighed its lowest branches open
like a woman lifting her skirts,
to reveal you lying there, chin to knee,
gasping like a thing newborn —
first breathing, we all learn to cry.

HEATHER MACLEOD

Shaman
In memory of Simeon Beeds

Old man rise from your grave.
I spread wild flowers and feathers
over your land.
I dance wildly, my arms spread out
and sometimes I scream.
I only manage to make it rain.

I bend my body pretending to be old.
I hold sticks in my arms
and toss them by the river's edge.
"Come on old man," I whisper,
"get up from your bed."

I do cartwheels and sing:
Michael row your boat ashore ...
and kill muskox and caribou.
I think the smell of blood
will tickle his nose.

Shaman, rise from your grave
covered in MTV and twinkies,
kick the dust from your feet.
Old man there is still
living in your bones

but even as I speak
he flutters to dusk,
settling on my boots.
I kick him from me and ride
my Harley into the debris of the future.

HEATHER MACLEOD

The Old Hag-Woman

Old hag-woman built her home in trees.
Lived by the easiest methods possible.
Old hag just wants to be free.
She says: Take a lesbian lover,
only another woman can know your cunt.

I skip pebbles on the lake
and make sounds like the crows.
The beaks sharp and long and they are
so impossibly black.
No one knows I am Indian unless I tell them
but they call my brother Chief.
He grows his black hair long
and I like to touch the curls
that fall down his back.
In the summer he wears charcoal
under his eyes and down his nose
and tells me he will scare away the sun.
It won't matter if I darken my skin.
I am still blond and my eyes
will remain green. My brother laughs at me
and tells me that I am white.

I climb the trees in the Shuswap forest
until Old hag-woman finds me.

Her back is bent and her hair
whiter than my skin. She just laughs at me.
She talks about my father,
she tells me things no one knows but me.
I say it was the whisky that made
him the way he was. She just shakes her head.
When I leave her I decide to live simply
and I refuse for the longest time
to take anyone into my bed.

CHARLOTTE DE CLUE

Blanket Poem #2
The Pox

The women keen
songs that I hear
as if they were late winter wind
coming down from cedars
biting my face
my hands
clutching the small infant
zhin-ga zhin-ga
tiny little one.
I won't let go of him
they tell me "let go of him"
he has melted into my breasts
part of me that way
he is my hand
holding his
his tiny fingers
"let go" they say
and fold his arm inside the shroud
and wrap him tight
like mama taught *me* to do
and then put him in the babyboard
she would tie him
big brother dangling tiny bells
above baby brother's head

"hang them high" mama would say
"make him reach for them
with his eyes
with his ears
soon he will walk."
　The women lick their fingertips
dip them in red dye
paint red spots on the white linen
mama wails like the wind coming up
cries and sways
wind through willow.
　The men lower him
quickly
ground loosens
folds over him like mama's arms
quickly
quickly
as if burying a secret
"he is still contagious, sister"
they say
"you don't want to be sick."
　My face in auntie's shoulder
rain
rain coming down
sweetwater rain
coming down
earth water rain
coming down
swelling

mama's belly
rising
water
sweet water flowing
mama's voice covering my ears
closing my eyes
"let go now, sister
let him sleep."

KATHRYN BELL

Ester

woman in the sun
   you are old
growing younger,

With the song the gull sings
   fleeting past your body
   of summer earth,

   i see winter approaching
   Seeing the chill in your eyes,
   i huddle close into your fire . . .
   listening to the echo of your steps

   falling silent in the snow

KATHRYN BELL

Cordell, OK, 1950

Gypsy and his spirits move silently
      in the windless night

   into the Circle

      no protection at their backs,

the movement of the blind dog
      carrying luck in white teeth flashing —

Running free

   i stalk the moving shadows

      under the nightsky,
smelling the closeness of earth,

   weaving me into memories

   of jagged animals
lurking in stone shelters.

LEONA HAMMERTON

Musical Scream

sometimes
life hurts
sometimes
i want to scream out
against injustice
in any form
violated rights
a beaten woman
a starving child
sometimes
i would like to scream
to vent my anger
in a primal scream of rage
loud enough
to drown
to stop the bombing
and gunfire
in this war torn world
gunfire
so people can drive
two city blocks
to accumulate enormous fat deposits
by raping the forests
ravaging the countrysides
for a pretty gem-stone

set
on sacred pink gold
stolen goods
to wrap around another marriage
a mock ceremony
condemned
to a statistic of two to five years
wedding guests secretly place bets
as they smile
a greasy smile
and wipe their lips
to kiss the bride
i know
i know that my primal scream of rage
done just right
at precisely the right moment
will shock my world
into silence
expectation
ears straining
i know
that i will sense
the first musical notes
from deep within a secret part of me
musical notes that have such freedom
freedom to wail
in the longest drawn outcry
freedom to laugh
musical laughter

an offering to the celebration of life
to be danced through
exquisite turns and leaps
executed to wonderful music
of my own creation
only i can leap and twirl
to the special rhythm
that demands
a perfect pirouette
and a tinkling of laughter
as i join
with other dancers
in this
ballet of life

Victoria Lena Manyarrows

The Native Ones

i hear the wind blowing in the trees
  fall is coming, and so are the soldiers
mounted police marching in this land of ice
  approaching, coming closer to our homes, our lands
our elders being threatened by the stick and the gun

yesterday was not enough
it wasn't enough for you to kill us to take our lands
it wasn't enough for you to imprison us, trying to
silence us
it wasn't enough for you to steal our youth, wanting to
crush our culture

  and make us forget that we are the native ones
  the ones who lived here first
  and breathed with the earth
  and felt her joy, a joy we shared
  but today it seems lost
  hatred replacing the love
our people suffering the steady abuse, the steady attacks
  genocidal and heartless it is only expected
from a race of conquerors and selfish people
  we are not surprised

we are not surprised
when you come again, with your weapons
   and your words of hate
shouting to us as mohawk, muskogee
   cherokee and chickasaw
that we must leave our land
   and give it to you gladly

giving you what you want, when you want
   but we receive nothing

to you,
we are not human

VICTORIA LENA MANYARROWS

Braiding/Ribbons of Revolution

braiding is a way of joining strands
    of midnight & brown
    of auburn & gray
    of silver & white
    of red & black ribbons of revolution
still blowing in the wind

and don't forget the winds are daily
blowing through the palms on those warm shores
and the earth still shakes without notice
frightening the war-weary and hungry
reminding us how suddenly change can happen
votes taken, votes stolen by agents of the underworld
visiting from the north, the land of the dollar & broken
dreams
illusion & facade, Hollywood sets
and misses ready for revenge, if anyone should try
again
to stand up and speak out for freedom & truth
sovereignty & self-determination

      no nicaragua

in the north sovereignty is a dirty word
and dissent is dangerous

and treaties are lies, laws are lies
and braiding is what indians do
so braiding is banned, and long strands are shaved off
military style, so indian men can look like marines
imprisoned and isolated
waiting for shock treatments from the imposters of
freedom
white trash of america
enemies of life & the winds of change

in the north treaties are always broken
and treaties can be broken again
    and again
    and again
some say treaties are made to be broken
and braiding is out of fashion
but i'll still braid your ribbons of hope
joining those strands of strength & years
weaving us together as one
a revolution of red & black, green & brown
and the blue of the ocean & the yellow of the sun
a revolution of love & fire
passion, burning away silos & sickness
a world ailing, aching, and lost
re-seeding these lands with hope & dreams of a new day

MARCIE RENDON

jesus christ
wasn't born a woman
menstruation
would have kept him out of the
temple at age 12
he would have been
raped
hitch-hiking
from Bethlehem to Jerusalem
his nursing children
would have screamed
and starved
without milk for
40 days and 40 nites
the loaves and fish
would have been made
into hotdish
to serve a few more
nope
jesus christ
wasn't born a woman
he wouldn't have had
time to be crucified

MARCIE RENDON

she lived while others talked
in smokey pool halls and dusty bars
she lived while others talked
            in Denver she had a Navajo
      he asked, "can I buy you a drink?"
she said, "no, take me home."
            he was quite surprised, it wasn't even closing time
he loved her first husband out of her
in the foothills of the Rockies
Mountain Daylight
savings time
            in Mission, South Dakota, a brave Lakota
            dude
            tried to hold the whirlwind
            braid a 'flyin, laughin'
she danced across the prairies of Nebraska
Winnebago's stompin' time
Oklahoma oil wells called
49ers singin' time
            she lived while others talked
a Blackfoot up Montana way
took her home to meet his ma
it didn't take her very long
she decided she slept better in the car
she quit drinkin' down in Rosebud
somehow just lost the taste

but they continued talkin'
and she continued livin'
there was the full-blood from Ponemah
the hunter from Nett Lake
the blond-blue-eyed Shinabe from White Earth
the tradish from Mill Lac
at pow-wows
old women pointed leather lips her way
old men shook their staffs in shame
younger women grabbed their men
holdin' on for life
braid a flyin', laughin'
she danced into the nite
they gave her powers
she didn't know she had
they said she ground up elk horn
fed it to them on the sly
there was somethin' in her moccasin
or somethin' in her eye
braid a twirlin', laughin', she too wondered
why
braid a flyin', twirlin'
she lived while others talked.

MARCIE RENDON

my own grandmothers
have no names
their heroic actions
erased from history's page

in lessons to the world
the enemy has recorded
our greatest warriors' names

Crazy Horse, Sitting Bull, Geronimo, Chochise
resistance fighters all

and yet
my own grandmothers have no names
their heroic actions
erased from history's page

MARCIE RENDON

you see this body
i mean
do you see this body?
>legs, are you a leg man?
>let me tell you 'bout these beautiful legs,
>leg man
they have walked and stood and squatted

walked across this nation on the Trail of Tears
stood firm at Wounded Knee
squatted to give birth to all humanity

>oh yes leg man, these sure are some
>beautiful legs

and you, hey you over there
you like ass, you an ass man?
>let me tell you about this ass

it's been kicked and shoved and beat
Nazi's, nuns, KKK, U.S. soldiers

>feel it man, soft and round, good as new
>some beautiful ass huh?

you see this body
i mean
do you see this body?

hey man, you over there
see this smile and flashing eyes
        pretty smile and flashing eyes
        sure can turn your head

hey man, let me tell you 'bout this pretty smile
        and flashing eyes

got me cross the Berlin Wall
free passage on a ship outta Nam
fed my kids quicker than the welfare line

amazing smile and flashing eyes
turned you head

        just long enough

MARCIE RENDON

this woman that i am becoming
is a combination of the woman that i am
and was
this journey backward will help me to walk forward

sister
the rape of a woman
is the rape of the earth
the rape of a child
the rape of the universe

as i voice these words
i watch you turn your well-kept
sunday morning presence
from this body that is heavy
with emotion
surviving
i have violated
your myths of motherhood
knowing full well
some silent summer night
my daughter's screams
will invade your
peaceful sleep
as they echo off the stars
some dew-covered morning

you will walk outside
to gather strawberries
and find instead
a gaping cavern
the ultimate rape
having finally been committed

sister
hear me now
let us take this journey
together

Fiction

EDNA H. KING

Taino Woman-Child

*"Later they came swimming to the ships' launches where
we were and brought us parrots and cotton thread in balls and
javelins and many other things, and they traded them to us for
other things which we gave them, such as small glass beads and
bells. In sum, they took everything and gave of what they had
willingly. But it seemed to me that they were a people very
poor in everything. All of them go around as naked as their
mothers bore them; and the women also, although I did not see
more than one quite young girl."*

I SHUT MY EYES FOR A MOMENT, SEARCHING FOR A SURGE
of energy. Instead, I began to drift towards sleep. A
sudden rustle of sound from across the room startled
me, and my eyes flew open. Peering at me from outside
my window stood an unclothed girl. Her face tear-
stained.

I helped her inside asking, "Are you alright?"

I worried that she had been abused and the abuser
was pursuing her. Hustling her aside I pulled the curtains shut and wrapped a bathrobe around her. "Would
you like me to call the police?" I offered, "Ambulance?
Anyone?"

She blinked.

She was a Native child, but no one I recognized.
"Could I telephone your mother for you?" I added wondering if she had recently moved into the neighbour-

hood.

Huge tears rolled down from her eyes.

The eyes. Hypnotically, they bore through me. Suddenly it seemed as though this child and I had known each other forever.

She told me her name, but because of my ignorance in linguistics I had quickly forgotten it. She was thirteen years old, and had been in search of her older sister, who had left the family village mysteriously. She also claimed her family belonged to the Taino Nation.

I felt a shiver run through my body. The Tainos. I knew who they were, and what their fate had been. Their population reached its peak a little over five centuries ago. Somehow, I knew that this woman-child was not from this place, nor from this time.

The language she spoke from her tongue should have been very different from mine. But, the Spirit World works mysteriously. It makes the impossible possible and whatever communication problems she and I would have had ceased to exist that night.

Taino Woman-child. That's what I began to call her. She was tall, thin, and beautiful. Her hair was as long and as black as my own. Her eyes were a deep, dark brown. One might have mistaken us for sisters if we had walked down the street side by side.

Taino Woman-child. She needed no machine, no box, no capsule to visit me. It was only the will of something much more powerful than either of us.

Taino Woman-child. From the island of Guanahani.

She lived with her mother, father, and several brothers and sisters. Many cousins, aunts, and uncles lived on her island. And all of the old women were her grandmothers and all of the old men her grandfathers.

She spoke of the neighbouring islands near her home and the trading that went on between them. Cotton threads for a woven basket; a parrot for red dye. Necessity outweighed luxury on a number of occasions.

They believed the Great Mystery had something wonderful in store for them. They obeyed the ancient stories and laws that spoke of honour, faith, and trust. The unwritten laws of nature and Mother Earth were very much respected. Anything good, or anything bad, that happened to them, or around them, were the acts of the Great Mystery.

Taino Woman-Child. She spoke of colourful birds, and fish that danced on the waters, of sweet smelling herbs and delicious fruits, about diving into high salty waves and climbing tall exotic trees.

I told her how I wished I could visit her in her time and her place. But my new friend hung her head and began to stare despairingly at her feet.

I walked to her, sat beside her, and placed my hand on her shoulder. She looked into my eyes and I could see hundreds of years of pain. Then she leaned her head against my shoulder and wept.

I consoled her for a while, telling her that whatever had happened to her was past and should be forgotten. She looked at me with teary eyes and blinked. Through trembling lips, she whispered, "You can't forget!" Sobbing, she added, "You have to remember, if not for me, then for your grandchildren." She looked deep into my eyes, and by some magical exchange of time, I began to see things as I have never seen them before.

I envisioned a new place. In this new place it was also night. Grandmother Moon stood with her brothers and sisters, the stars. Her reflection quivered on top of the vast waters. Waves slapped the shoreline to the beat of a soundless drum. I could smell each salty white cap as they touched the shoreline before retreating. I watched trees sway in the cool breeze and could taste the tropical air that made them dance. The surroundings enveloped me and I felt a certain calm. I knew then that I was visiting the home of my friend Taino Woman-child.

I could see myself lying on the floor of a *rancho* among strangers I assumed were Taino Woman-child's family. I could hear the even breathing of some of her family members as they slept in hammocks, while others lay on the floor beside me. Inhaling deeply, I could taste the herbal scents that came from drying plants hanging from the ceiling over our heads. Then I looked towards my new friend. Like two secret sharing girls she and I looked at one another and smiled.

In one quick motion, Taino Woman-child placed a finger to her lips. "Shhh, listen," she advised.

We could hear the hushed voices of men.

On our knees, we crawled away from her sleeping family.

Beyond the thicket we could see the shadows of the men around a fire. I knew that it must have been the village warriors for every Nation had warriors. Taino Woman-child moved slowly, careful not to awaken the rest. I followed.

We sat behind bushes, moving branches to get a closer look. Her eyes began to light up and her face broke into a smile. She pointed her head in their direction. "Do you see the man closest to the fire?" I nodded. "That's the man I will marry, at the time the birds begin to migrate north."

I gazed at him. He was a handsome, muscular youth. She must be so proud of him, and I told her so, adding that they made a lovely couple.

She nodded, smiling proudly. "Together, we plan to have many children. I told him I wanted all sons so they could be strong warriors like their father. He wants daughters who will be just like me."

Then, Taino Woman-child put a hand to her ear to hear their voices more clearly. She could make out the words they spoke and translated them to me.

Her face quickly changed expression. In awe she explained to me, "There are huge vessels near the shore. My uncle thinks the Great Mystery has sent a messenger."

"Our shaman said that whatever the vessels are they are sure to bring only evil. He said that we should be wary of them."

I watched as she settled on her knees, then copied her.

"The men can't decide what the vessels mean and why they are here," she whispered to me.

"They are like no other and can not be from the neighbouring islands for Grandfather knows of no people who could build canoes that size."

"They've decided that when Sun awakens a greeting party will go to them. They will take offerings of peace."

Taino Woman-child covered her mouth to stifle a laugh. "They cannot decide what gifts to take to them," she said. "My man thinks everyone should give the same thing. My uncle thinks that idea is silly. He thinks it would be more appropriate to make offerings of spiritual medicines."

I shivered. I knew, in my heart who the occupants of those ships were. But, I could not bring myself to speak out. In the back of my mind I could hear Taino Woman-child's voice say, "Grandfather thinks that everyone should give something that is very valuable to each of us and share it with them, and by sharing with them something personal we are giving them a piece of ourselves." My mind began to reel.

The sun rose quickly that day, or so it seemed. As word spread about the strange vessels, small groups of villagers began to assemble along the shore. There were grandmothers, grandfathers, children, and small babies. Hushed voices, pointing fingers, curious onlookers stared toward the ocean. The warriors began to take charge, pointing towards the heart of the island.

Taino Woman-child said, "Our warriors are ordering

all elders, women, and children to hide in the middle of thick brush, at the centre of Guanahani. They don't want anyone to return until they know everything is safe. At that time, a search party will bring them back.

"Grandmother is worried about the safety of the men. The Shaman has ordered all warriors to arm themselves with spears. Grandfather doesn't like the idea but he will not condemn anyone who wishes to be armed."

Then she crouched low to the ground. "Shh, get down closer to Earth. Don't let anyone know we are hiding here."

I was so unsure of what to think. All of those who were ordered to leave did so, with little argument. That is, all those except Taino Woman-child. "Aren't you going to follow your family?" I asked her.

"No," she said quietly. "Besides, I still have family members waiting to greet the strangers." She paused for a moment, then added, "I just want to see what they look like." And she waited.

When the others were out of sight, everything began to move quickly. The warriors began to get in canoes and paddle towards the vessels. Lean, pale men began to peer over the sides of the ships. Some of them began to lower smaller vessels into the ocean.

I sat still and afraid, feeling helpless. I recognized the ship's Admiral more by how he dressed and how the others gathered around him than by his own physical appearance. He was very much the politician, a description not found in the history books. I shivered as he trod up the shore and planted the cross, the cross that would change the course of history for every indigenous person in the Americas.

And, I knew every word he spoke, though I don't know how, for he was speaking Spanish. He said a prayer and claimed the land for King Ferdinand and Queen Isabella. I couldn't contain myself any longer and began to rise to stop him.

Taino Woman-child clutched my arm, and squeezed it. "There isn't anything you could say or do to stop this," she said. "No one can see you, or hear you. Only I."

"Then stop him," I begged. "Warn your family to stop him."

"I can't," she said. "Because this is the will of the Great Mystery." Then, she quietly added, "Someone has to learn from what is happening here." At that, she stood and walked towards them, unashamed of her unclothed body, and stubbornly sat on the sandy shore alone.

I stood in the background, watching, as they all exchanged gifts. Glass Beads and trinkets for valuable personal possessions. It was the beginning of unfair misconceptions, of unfair tradings, of an unfair advantage of trust.

I watched as Taino Woman-child was approached by a sailor, who adorned her with a beaded necklace, and put his arm around her thirteen year old body, and hugged her, gently at first, then tighter, as if he owned her.

I knew her father would, through courtesy, allow her

to marry the sailor, rather than the young man from her village. And I knew Taino Woman-child's man would resent the adjoining. Somehow, I knew that, after a few months, when the Admiral was to return to Spain, Taino Woman-child's young man would be one of those unwilling passengers going to Spain as a slave, while his "future" wife stayed with the sailor. And those realizations hit me hard, and I mourned for her, and for him.

Then everything became fast and distorted, as in dream sequences. Women and girls were being raped and ravished. Babies were bludgeoned. And the warriors, who vowed to protect those they loved, soon became victims themselves. Those that survived, began leaping into the ocean's depth, and swam under ledges beneath the islands, to die rather then submit to slavery and pain. Over 495 years later, in a science lab, their skeletons would be probed over inch by inch as scientists scrambled to discover why these beautiful people would choose to commit mass suicide.

Historically, I knew, that torture and murder took place, not as much from Columbus's first voyage, but from the others that followed. But for me, in this vision, everything occurred quickly, brightly, and loudly.

The hopelessness and helplessness of the historical realities gripped my soul. And, I begged Taino Woman-child to allow me to return home.

With a heavy heart and a heavy head, I lay facedown on my own comfortable bed. I quickly sat up and wiped my brow. Exhausted, I walked to the bathroom sink and splashed water onto my face.

I looked at my reflection in the mirror and rubbed my eyes.

Staring behind me I could make out the image of Taino Woman-child. I turned to look for her, but she was not standing there. I looked back into the mirror and her image was more clear.

"Do you see what has happened?" she said to me. "My people were real people, just like you, and your neighbours, and your family and friends. We had feel ings, dreams and ideas. We were not savages or animals." And then tears filled her eyes.

"I knew you were, Taino Woman-child," was all that I could say as she began to fade.

I felt saddened as her image disappeared. But, her departure symbolized to me the need to secure mechanisms necessary to consecrate the ways of life of Indigenous people. The experience gained from the past five hundred years, and the fate of thousands of First Nations people have been valuable lessons to ensure the survival of others.

The Diary of Christopher Columbus's First Voyage to America, 1492-1493, Abstracted by Fray Bartoleme de las Casas, transcribed and translated by Oliver Dunn and James E. Kelley, Jr. Norman: University of Oklahoma Press, 1989.

Rancho: Hut-like structure. Bamboo poles in four-corners, held up light covered roof. In the Caribbean at time of contact it would have been wall-less.

LEE MARACLE

The Laundry Basket

THE LAUNDRY BASKET IS FULL AGAIN. THE WICKER basket is old, its sides bursting in spots. She mentally promises to buy a new one — when her financial situation has altered. Number 42 on the old list of priorities. She had forgotten how, but somehow the basket had been bent so that it leaned to the side instead of standing up straight. Soiled shirts and overalls formed a mound on top. A stiff little sock sat perched on the edge of the clothes, barely hanging onto the rest of the laundry. Nothing seemed to be holding it onto the stack. She shut the bathroom door on the laundry scene very carefully so as not to jar the sock loose. She ignored the little voice inside her calling her to tend to the laundry.

It's midday. The sun overhead whispers pale shadowless light. The yard outside the window is bright, but inside it's a little dull. Only morning light shines into the old living room. First draft is done and she pulls the last sheet from the typewriter, then pours herself a coffee. *Coffee. Poison really.* But she has so precious few vices. *No excuse.* It's kind of like the laundry in reverse. She knows it should be done, but it's midday, too late to begin a major overhaul of the family wardrobe. She should just do it. Coffee is poison, she should just quit drinking it, but she neither does what she ought to nor stops doing what she ought not to. It seems misbehaviour is her reward for freeing herself of domination.

The voice nags on: *the kids will need clean clothes for school*. Turn the damn things inside out, this isn't the reserve. There was a time when we weren't so goddamned concerned about other people's opinions. This isn't 1950.

She tells herself to shut up and starts proofing her last piece. The walls pulse. The floor starts to sway, the footprint in the wallpaper squeezes his memory from behind its gaudy pictures.

My mother held a job and did the laundry, too, the quality of his voice changed. During his endless complaining about her unwillingness to work and work and work, his voice had been loud and arrogant. Now in its dreamy memory state it possessed a mocking purr as though he knew she was not keeping up with the holy duties of motherhood from wherever in the world he was.

Get out she threatens the silent walls as though he were really there. The very pattern of the paper seems to hold her past in tact. He chose the paper, like the laundry basket — wicker is natural, he had said against her desire for plastic. *Yeah, natural and uncleanable.* She now remembered how the damn thing got its wow in it. She had washed it in hot water and the wicker had warped. She was mad all over again. And the wallpaper. She had thought he must have been a repressed nurse when he wanted food, loud and raw, to adorn the kitchen. She hadn't said anything at the time, but now tears rested just behind her eyes stubbornly threatening to roll out onto the machine. She could have said no. No to the wallpaper, no to the wicker, but she knew she could not say no to having to do the laundry, mother the children and him, and somehow that seemed so pathetic. Pathetic because she had lived with it for so long and he had left without ever realizing how tyrannous he was.

She looked up at the old clock. Two hours. *I will still have time* she soothed herself. *What am I doing, he's gone but his voice still dictates my every mood. It hangs thick in the air, loud like the paper.* The words are whispered out loud. They try to squeeze themselves between the designs of the paper trying to shove the memory back into the grapes, vegetables, and bread hanging off the plain white paper. *Whoever heard of bright gold grapes, yellow bread, or sharp green tomatoes and carrots.* That remark erased his presence.

Her hand is still clutching the cup of cool coffee. On the side of the cup is written "decision-maker." The lip of the cup was well-chipped. "Hepatitis can be contracted from chipped stoneware," she had read somewhere and reminded herself to add new dishes to her list of priorities. Number 43. She had gotten it for a birthday in the days when things were going well between them. Well, for him that is. To be truthful, things had been magical for both of them in those first few years. She had done her household duties with enthusiasm, actually believing that her obligations as wife were her source of joy. Decision-maker. The irony of the gift now struck her.

In fact, he had left most of the household decision-making to her in those years. It was when she had stepped out of the bounds of orthodoxy that he had "put his foot down," or rather, began putting the back of his hand across her face. She wanted to remember the precise moment, the pivotal point of her change.

The clock rolled backward across her memory and Choklit Park came into view. She was staring at them all: her husband, her two children, and a friend of theirs, all roughhousing, sliding, and swinging on the toys at the park. From the hill she could see False Creek and the memory of Khatsalano rolled into focus. He was staring across the water from a hillside in North Vancouver, pining to be buried in his lost homeland.

She was a little girl, just like her eldest son, but instead of swinging on swings or hanging from bars, she was listening to an old man.

The children and her husband receded. Silence, but for old Khatsalano's voice and finally, the picture of the park changed. Vancouver was still so new then. Bush adorned the edges of the inlet right up to the sugar refinery. Now it's roadway and park — Brighton Park and deep sea vessels. The Vancouver Hotel bragged about being the tallest building; now you can't even see it from the other side. False Creek was just a Marina and a barrel company during the last days of Khatsalano, now it is the most densely populated residential area in the city. Prime real estate. It was funny to hear them say that as though land could be likened to beef — prime real estate, prime rib roast. Khatsalano could not write. His face faded and the children returned.

She had made her decision then. It had been unspoken even in her mind, but shortly after that she had gone out and brought an unabridged dictionary and had began the tedious process of looking up parts of speech — English grammar construction. She had been noting them in an exercise book for some time. On the trail to recover language she had come across a host of interesting words and she played with her thoughts in little scribbles...

The crunching sound of mail sliding through the old slot breaks the pattern of her thoughts. More bills. Reluctantly, she moves to the floor where the bent envelopes sit in disarray. There just isn't a way to toss letters through a skinny slot without crunching them up and having them land in a position of indignity. *Disarray, like the damn laundry, the wallpaper, and my life.*

The hum of the typewriter overtop the soft shuffling of the envelopes reminds her that she had chosen to purchase a writing machine instead of a washing machine. *Not very thrifty. Too late now.* She is broke and considers pawning the typewriter. *What would it be like not to be able to kick out story after story for the rejection of editor after editor? I'll die if I don't keep pecking, believing.*

The last scene between Grant and her returned. Papers, piled one on top of the other, crinkled up in the tub and the match that set fire to them all. A scream had rolled out from the bottom of her feet, grew in intensity threatening to swallow her. It had stopped at her heart. It was too big. The howl snapped her attention.

You want to burn this do you? You want to burn my life.

*You want to burn the inside of me, the soul of me. Burn me.
Me?* and she had reached into the laundry basket and
hauled shirt after shirt out and then thrown them onto the
paper pyre in the tub. He yelled. Momentarily caught by
surprise, he had hesitated long enough for the edges of
the soiled shirts to burn. He tried to rescue the shirts by
pouring water on the fire, then backhanded her. It
seemed like a single motion. It had been enough.

It didn't take him long to disappear. She had been
surprised at the swiftness of her next few decisions. The
injunction, the charges, the inability of the police to find
him, then the divorce. A whirlwind storm of decision.
She had not realized how devoted she was to her stories.
What had brought it all on? Most of her pieces had been
harmless little bits of entertainment for the kids. Some she
gave away to friends.

She remembered Sara. Sara was moving back home
to take care of teenaged children whose father had given
up trying to raise them. The customs of divorce had all
changed in the last while. Men were gaining custody of
young children, then as the problems of biochemical
teenage revolution fell on them, they were returning them
to their mothers.

She wanted to give Sara something, something in-
tensely personal, something of her soul. A story that was
close to her heart. Sara knew about publishers and had
sent the story to some magazine. They wanted it. That's
all it took. The possibility of turning her life and the lives
of hundreds of other unknowns to account had inspired

her. Inspired her in a way no man, woman, or child could.

Scribbling became an obsession. When she wasn't scribbling she was reading. Story after story came off the typewriter in clean neat rows. They circled through her insides and became part of her. His rage, his omnipresence, shrunk as her passion for her own words grew. He objected. She resisted. Sneaking about during the day, she wrote furtively, secretly. She saved time by not caring so much about housework. Wall-washing was sacrificed for writing. Deleting daily floor washing added to writing time. She took to washing dishes only during the half hour before he returned home from work. She accumulated time the way misers save money. Moment by moment, penny by penny. She let the laundry pile up week after week until there were no clothes left in the house and she absolutely had to wash or get caught.

Get caught. How absurd her lifestyle seemed now. Get caught, like somehow her lack of devotion to housework were some crime. She had felt guilty leaving the poor old socks in the basket until she had no choice but to haul them to the laundromat. *Poor old socks.* Still, she scribbled and scribbled. She sent envelope after envelope out to magazines. She bought a Canadian Writer's guide. Very few of her imagination's journeys seemed to fit into the editorial plans of magazine publishers. Romance among indigenous people is so subtle that white Canadians would not recognize a love story about us if they fell on it. Still, she carried on. Most times she never heard from the people again, but once in a while an editor's note would come back "too narrow a genre, not remarkable, take the drinking out, the violence is too raw for our audience, no one will purchase a magazine with stories about child sexual abuse." The answer's spurred her on. No one said the writing was bad. It was her choice of subject they didn't care for. *Someday, our lives will interest you, Canada, and I will have a host of angels just waiting for you to read.*

The stories got closer, sharper, more vivid, more honest. Finally, he crept into them. His rage, the stupidity of feminine bondage and male dominance rolled out on the crisp white sheets. She had crouched the essence of him in fiction, but he was still recognizable. He went to work as usual, suspecting nothing. He returned home and found her as available and almost as devoted as usual. He was smug about his victory over her silly obsession. He even made fun of her dreams by perusing the entertainment section of the paper and reading reviews of new works.

"Wouldn't you like to be one of these guys, Marla. Look here, another new book. Of course, this one is written by a *real* writer." She cringed, remained silent, and finally grew distant, almost immune to his remarks.

One Friday, he had returned an hour or so early and found the lot. She hadn't been there at first. She wondered what his face looked like when he read her story, saw himself, and began crumpling sheet after sheet. She wondered if he had paced at all about the kitchen, looking for the right receptacle, before finally deciding to use the tub. The tub. It was in the tub that she had helped her children burn pictures of their nightmares. Maybe it was all a nightmare for him, a white man, to see his Indian bride become one of the pampered literati of Canada. The sickening notion that he had fallen in love with her because he wanted someone he could feel superior to struck her.

She had come back from the next door neighbours' in time to watch the lot burn. She saw herself going up in smoke. The word fire ignited her insides. Her shirts, his precious shirts, the ones he so carefully selected, tailored to fit, as though they expressed his very soul, joined her words. She had watched her hands commit the crime and in some strange way had felt lusty for the first time in a long while.

Even though his backhand had hurt her she had wanted to laugh — a sultry, deep-throated, full and lusty laugh. It scared her now. It dawned on her, maybe he had figured it out. Maybe he had become so incensed because he associated her dwindling sensuousness with her increased writing. It felt creepy, sexually perverse, for him to sense something about the relationship of her sensuality to writing before she had come to realize it. She felt as though she had just been told that someone was watching her undress every night without her knowing.

Her hands stopped shuffling. They had rested themselves on a cheque. The cheque was waiting for her to pay attention. She tore the thing open, letting the other letters fall to the floor. "Edie's Courtship" had made it. The cheque and the prospect of a second hand Hoover washer crowded out the memories. She waved the cheque in triumph. The laugh she couldn't utter under her ex-husband's backhand burst out.

The old station wagon she had brought with her last cheque stood out front, lonely from lack of use. She grabbed her keys and climbed in, ground the beast into gear, and headed for "Joe's Used Appliance" yard at the end of the alley. Joe liked seeing her come in. She never bought anything, but he liked seeing her anyway. She was glorious. Thin, reedy, big-eyed, and full of smiles. Unconsciously, he drew a breath and held in his gut before swaggering in her direction.

"She's on a roll, Joe. Money. A cheque. I'll take that Hoover over there, if you will trust me with this cheque." She was laughing, looking lovelier than ever.

Joe joined her. He took a look at the cheque. "McClelland and Stewart, not bad. Are they going to publish the whole book?"

"The whole damn thing" she answered. "This is a lot of money. I better make sure I can change it." She hugged him. He spun her around.

The Hoover stood saying *buy me*. She felt a little weepy. No more rude laundresses breaking her reading up to tell her, "Your MA-chine IS ready."

From the till he mentioned her needing the dryer. This one was not much good without the other. "Oh

God," she thought and the grating stress of decision-making was upon her again. New wallpaper and a table and chairs or a damn dryer. Joe was right, the little washer wasn't much good without the dryer. But the wallpaper that hid his image in the harmless, gaudy print of food would have to stay if she took the dryer. Hot rage boiled inside. She suddenly wondered how a man could spend thirty bucks a crack on dozens of shirts while his family went without a table and chairs and his wife rolled off once a week, harnessed to a shopping cart, to a laundromat whose laundress could hardly tolerate her race, and he drove to work in his new car?

The portrait of her kitchen with a piece of plywood nailed to an old drum sitting in the middle returned to her. She wanted to cry.

She stared hard at Joe. Within the pale of his skin, his blue eyes, the mass of light brown hair playing on his face rested the answer. She had half a notion to ask him. His joy for her told her not to. He would never be able to understand the question, she was not even sure how to frame it. She felt he was at the bottom of her ex-husband's obsession with tailored shirts and his own transport taking precedence over family needs. He had never brought any of his work mates to their house. It dawned on her, he had never intended to let anyone he respected know what his wife looked like. Hot shame crowded her mind. Joe knows. Joe's people know. She told herself that this was ridiculous, how could Joe be blamed for her ex-husband's quirks? She hated saying that: *ex-husband,* as though you could never divorce the memory of marriage.

The courtroom scene of her divorce returned. She recalled the judge, relived the solemnity of the moment. He was old, white. His voice filled the room, like speaker of the bighouse, but it was cold. He held a silly hammer in his hand — a gavel, she now knew. She had wanted him to give her some instructions, to say something profound. Instead he simply granted her a divorce in unadorned flat language and then dismissed her with his gavel. Her husband had not contested the divorce or her application for custody. No complications except the tight feeling inside her that wanted to say: *Excuse me, I just divorced your entire race, your honour, wouldn't you like to comment on that? I chucked out his entire lineage as a possible source of comfort in the hereafter, don't you resent that for just a moment.*

"Are you o.k.?" She woke up to Joe's face looking curiously at her. She wondered how long her thoughts had taken. Long enough for Joe to notice anyway.

"I gotta stop doing this. I was just daydreaming, conjuring up my next story. Are you divorced, Joe?"

"Oh yeah. Who isn't these days?" He got shy, less brassy, like he was hoping there was something for him in question. She decided not to pursue it any further. She couldn't tell him that he was a nice guy, but she had already divorced his entire race. Best not to get into a position where she would have to tell the truth if the truth was too ugly for the listener to understand.

"Put the dryer in the wagon too, Joe," then she

turned to leave. She didn't get far. Joe called out after her, wondering how she thought she was going to get the dryer from the car to her apartment.

"We'll manage" she answered, cautiously curt. She smiled back gratefully, but carried on. At the house she had to wait until her boys returned. Between the three of them, the assistance of an Egyptian jack and a whole lot of grunting effort, planning, re-planning and making judicious use of muscle and leverage smarts; the three of them managed to get the two machines into the apartment.

Joe had given her change for the cheque. She clung to the bills, a ten and a twenty. She decided to order pizza. "Go to hell walls" she murmured while dailing 222-2222.

While waiting for the pizza man, the two boys loaded the little Hoover and turned it on. Another milestone. She hadn't thought of that. It never occurred to her that for the boys, laundry was not looked upon us "women's work," wifely drudgery not fit for male consumption. It was new and they wanted to be part of it.

"Ooh, yuk, this one must be yours" the older one said to the little one holding up the stiff sock which had clung musically to the mound earlier. They roared with laughter.

"Killer socks," the little one answered.

She leaned against the bathroom doorway. The hum of the typewriter distracted her. She hadn't turned it off when she left. *Hydro excessiveness*, she chided herself, then shut if off. *Sun Dogs*, her new title stared at her. "*Sun Dogs*. If you make it, the wallpaper is next".

JANET BEAVER

Vision Quest

THE GIRL WAS PACING IMPATIENTLY, BACK AND FORTH, on the sandy beach. The waves were washing on the shore like thundering buffalo. For days she had been here on her vision quest but nothing had happened. She was becoming restless. Nervously slapping her thigh, waiting for the vision that would answer all of her questions.

In the distance, down the beach, she saw a large turtle emerging from the ocean. She walked over and said to the turtle, "Are you here for my vision quest?"

The turtle replied, "No, my daughter, I am here to lay my eggs in the warm sand."

"But I've been sitting here for days and no vision has appeared," the girl cried.

"Well," the turtle said, "what have you given in order that you may receive this vision?"

"I have given nothing" the girl replied. "I am here to receive, not to give."

"Oh, but you must always give if you wish to receive," the turtle said. "That is the way of things."

So the girl proceeded to build a fire on the beach. When the fire was hot, the girl threw tobacco and sage and boughs of cedar as gifts to the Great Spirit. Still no vision appeared.

Meanwhile, the turtle had labouriously crawled up

the beach and was digging a large nest in the warm sand with her strong back legs. The girl walked over to the turtle and said, "Look, I've given the Great Spirit tobacco and sage and cedar and I've still had no vision."

"Instead of pacing around, back and forth like a caged wolf, you should just sit down and be quiet," the turtle said.

The girl did this and as her breathing quieted and she began to relax, she closed her eyes. She heard the sound of the water in the ocean and it was as though cooling water was flowing down over her whole body and she heard the song of the ocean coming to her on the wind.

She heard, as if for the first time in her life, the crackling of the burning cedar boughs as they were eaten by the flames. She could smell their essence on the wind. She gave thanks to the Great Spirit for the fire. Meegwetch.

She could hear the waves crashing on the shore and the sea began to talk to her, telling her of its family, of all the creatures that called the sea home, of life and death and life again in a never ending circle.

She could smell the seaweed and the tangy salt air. She could hear the whales breaching with their new calves in tow in the ocean off the beach. She could hear the dolphins chattering to one another as they played in the waves. She gave thanks to the Great Spirit for the water. Meegwetch.

As she listened, the sky began to murmur in her ear. It told her about its family of creatures that called the sky home. She heard the gulls calling to each other overhead. She heard the osprey as he dove into the ocean after the fish. She heard the eagle's cry as it searched for food for its young. She filled her lungs with the cool fresh air of the sky. She gave thanks to the Great Spirit for the sky. Meegwetch.

Before too long, the girl could hear a bear lumbering through the forest behind her. She had come to take up her post beside the river that drained into the sea to fish for salmon. Two cubs bounded out of the forest after her, bawling for their breakfast. Mother Earth was speaking to her, telling her about the family of creatures that called Mother Earth home. Mother Earth gently explained about the circle of life — about life and death and rebirth. She gave thanks to the Great Spirit for Mother Earth. Meegwetch.

Gently, a warm flood of understanding washed over the girl as she realized that all she had just experienced was her vision. She understood now, that life, all of life, is sacred. She now understood about the circle of life and death, give and take. She could see the circle of life hanging like a web of gold mesh, each link connected to many others, each link an essential element of the whole.

She had spent her whole life up until now so busy with the process of living that she hadn't actually lived. Here she was now, in this place, in this time, and she didn't even know where she had been. She took a solemn vow that, from this day forward, she would live each day as if it were the only day. She would give thanks each day to the Great Spirit for all of the other beings she shared this life with, and for the four elements of life: the earth, the air, the water, and fire.

The turtle stopped on her way back to the ocean. She stopped and said to the girl, "You have learned much, my daughter, on your vision quest. You must slow down so that you don't pass life by. In my life, I have learned that it matters not if you are flipped over onto your back. You are never helpless. You can do whatever you desire and you will always be part of the circle of life with all of the love, support, and energy of the fire, the water, the earth, and the sky." With that, the turtle swam into the sea and the girl began to sing her song of thanks to the Great Spirit.

BETH BRANT

This Is History
For Donna Goldleaf

L ONG BEFORE THERE WAS AN EARTH AND LONG BEFORE there were people called human, there was a Sky World.

On Sky World there were Sky People who were like us and not like us. And of the Sky People there was Sky Woman. Sky Woman was thought by the others to be content, but she had a peculiar trait — she had curiosity. She bothered the others with her questions, with wanting to know what lay beneath the clouds that supported her world. Sometimes she pushed the clouds aside and looked down through her world to the large expanse of blue that shimmered below. The others were tired of her peculiar trait and called her an aberration, a queer woman who asked questions, a woman who wasn't satisfied with what she had.

Sky Woman spent much of her time dreaming — dreaming about the blue expanse underneath the clouds, dreaming about floating through the clouds, dreaming about the blue colour and how it would feel to her touch. One day she pushed the clouds away from her and leaned out of the opening. She fell. The others tried to catch her hands and pull her back, but she struggled free and began to float downward. The Sky People watched her descent and agreed that they were glad to see her go.

She was a nuisance with her questions, an aberration, a queer woman who was not like them — content to walk the clouds undisturbed.

Sky Woman floated. The currents of wind played through her hair. She put out her arms and felt the sensation of air between her fingers. She kicked her legs, did somersaults, and explored the free, delightful feelings of flying. Faster, faster, she floated towards the blue shimmer that beckoned to her.

She heard a noise and looked to see a beautiful creature with black wings and white head flying close to her. The creature spoke, "I am Eagle. I have been sent to carry you to your new home."

Sky Woman laughed and held out her hands for Eagle to brush his wings against. He swooped under her and she settled on his back. They flew. They circled, glided, Sky Woman clutching the feathers of the great creature.

Sky Woman looked down at the blue colour, and rising from the expanse was a turtle. Turtle looked up at the flying pair and nodded her head. She dove into the waters and came up again with a muskrat clinging to her back. In Muskrat's paw was a clump of dark brown dirt scooped from the bottom of the sea. She laid it on Turtle's back and jumped back into the water. Sky Woman watched the creature swim away, her long tail skimming the top of the waves, her whiskers shining. Sky Woman watched as the dark brown dirt began to spread. All across Turtle's back the dirt was spreading, spreading and in this dirt green things were growing. Small green things, tall green things, and in the middle of Turtle's back, the tallest thing grew. It grew branches and needles, more branches and grew until it reached where Eagle and Sky Woman were hovering.

Turtle raised her head and beckoned to the pair. Eagle flew down to the Turtle's back and gently lay Sky Woman on the soft dirt. Then he flew to the very top of the White Pine tree and said, "I will be here, watching over everything that is to be. You will look to me as the harbinger of what is to happen. You will be kind to me and my people. In return I will keep this place safe." Eagle folded his wings and looked away.

Sky Woman felt the soft dirt with her fingers. She brought the dirt to her mouth and tasted the colour of it. She looked around at the green things and some were flowering with fantastic shapes. She stood on her feet and felt the solid back of Turtle beneath her. She marvelled at this wonderful place and wondered what she would do here.

Turtle swivelled her head and looked at Sky Woman with ancient eyes. "You will live here and make this a new place. You will be kind and you will call me Mother. I will make all manner of creatures and growing things to guide you on this new place. You will watch them carefully and from them, you will learn how to live. You will take care to be respectful and honourable to me. I am your Mother." Sky Woman touched Turtle's back and promised to honour and respect her. She lay down on

Turtle's back and fell asleep.

As she slept, Turtle grew. Her back became wider and longer. She slapped her tail and cracks appeared in her back. From these cracks came mountains, canyons were formed, rivers and lakes were made from the spit of Turtle's mouth. She shook her body and prairies sprang up, deserts settled, marshes and wetlands pushed their way through the cracks of Turtle's shell. Turtle opened her mouth and called. Creatures came crawling out of her back. Some had wings, some had four legs, six legs and eight. Some had no legs but slithered on the ground, some had no legs and swam with fins. These creatures crawled out of Turtle's back and some were covered with fur, some with feathers, some with scales, some with skins of beautiful colours. Turtle called again and the creatures found their voices. Some sang, some barked, some growled and roared, some had no voice but a hiss, some had no voice and rubbed their legs together to speak. Turtle called again. The creatures began to make homes. Some gathered twigs and leaves, others spun webs, some found caves, others dug holes in the ground. Some made the waters their home and some of these came up for air to breathe. Turtle shuddered and the new place was made a continent, a world.

Turtle gave a last look to the sleeping Sky Woman. "Inside you is growing a being who is like you and not like you. This being will be your companion. Together you will give names to the creatures and growing things. You will be kind to these things. This companion growing inside you will be called First Woman, for she will be the first of these beings on this earth. Together you will respect me and call me Mother. Listen to the voices of the creatures and communicate with them. This will be called prayer, for prayer is the language of all my creations. Remember me." Turtle rested from her long labour.

Sky Woman woke and touched herself. Inside her body she felt the stirring of another. She stood on her feet and walked the earth. She climbed mountains, she walked in the deserts, she slept in trees, she listened to the voices of the creatures and living things, she swam in the waters, she smelled the growing things that came from the earth. As she wandered and discovered, her body grew from the being inside her. She ate leaves, she picked fruit. An animal showed her how to bring fire, then threw himself in the flames that she might eat of him. She prayed her thanks, remembering Turtle's words. Sky Woman watched the creatures, learning how they live in community with each other, learning how they hunted, how they stored food, how they prayed. Her body grew larger and she felt her companion move inside her, waiting to be born. She watched the living things, seeing how they fed their young, how they taught their young, how they protected their young. She watched and learned and saw how things should be. She waited for the day when First Woman would come and together they would be companions, lovers of the earth, namers of all things, planters and harvesters, creators.

On a day when Sky Woman was listening to the

animals, she felt a sharp pain inside her. First Woman
wanted to be born. Sky Woman walked the earth, looking
for soft things to lay her companion on when she was
born. She gathered all day, finding feathers of the
winged-creatures, skins of the fur-bearers. She gathered
these things and made a deep nest. She gathered other
special things for medicine and magic. She ate leaves
from a plant that eased her pain. She clutched her magic
things in her hands to give her help. She prayed to the
creatures to strengthen her. She squatted over the deep
nest and began to push. She pushed and held tight to the
magic medicine. She pushed. The First Woman slipped
out of her and onto the soft nest. First Woman gave a cry.
Sky Woman touched her companion, then gave another
great push as her placenta fell from her. She cut the long
cord with her teeth as she had learned from the animals.
She ate the placenta as she had learned from the animals.
She brought First Woman to her breast as she had
learned, and First Woman began to suckle, drawing
nourishment and medicine from Sky Woman.

Sky Woman prayed, thanking the creatures for teaching her how to give birth. She touched the earth, thanking
Mother for giving her this gift of companion. Turtle shuddered, acknowledging the prayer. That day, Sky Woman
began a new thing. She opened her mouth and sound
came forth. Sounds of song. She sang and began a new
thing — singing prayers. She fashioned a thing out of
animal skin and wood. She touched the thing and it
resonated. She touched it again and called it drum. She

sang with the rhythm of her touching. First Woman suck-
led as her companion sang the prayers.

First Woman began to grow. In the beginning she lay
in her nest dreaming, then crying out as she wanted to
suckle. Then she opened her eyes and saw her companion
and smiled. Then she sat up and made sounds. Then she
crawled and was curious about everything. She wanted
to touch and feel and taste all that was around her. Sky
Woman carried her on her back when she walked the
earth, listening to the living things and talking with them.
First Woman saw all things that Sky Woman pointed out
to her. She listened to Sky Woman touch the drum and
make singing prayers. First Woman stood on her feet and
felt the solid shell of Turtle against her feet. The two
companions began walking together. First Woman made
a drum for herself and together, the companions made
magic by touching their drums and singing their prayers.

First Woman grew and as she grew, Sky Woman
showed her the green things, the animal things, the living
things and told her they needed to name them. Together
they began the naming. Heron, bear, snake, dolphin,
spider, maple, oak, thistle, cricket, wolf, hawk, trout,
goldenrod, firefly. They named together and in naming,
the women became closer and truer companions. The
living things that now had names moved closer to the
women and taught them how to dance. Together, they all
danced as the women touched their drums and made
their singing prayers. Together they danced. Together.
All together.

In time the women observed the changes that took place around them. They observed that sometimes the trees would shed their leaves and at other times would grow new ones. They observed that some creatures buried themselves in caves and burrows and slept for a long time, reappearing when the trees began their new birth. They observed that some creatures flew away for a long time, reappearing when the animals crawled from their caves and dens. Together, the companions decided they would sing special songs and different prayers when the earth was changing and the creatures were changing. They named these times seasons, and made new drums, sewn with feathers and stones. The companions wore stones around their necks, feathers in their hair and shells on their feet, and when they danced, the music was new and extraordinary. They prepared feasts at this time, asking the animals to accept their death. Some walked into their arrows, some ran away. The animals that gave their lives were thanked and their bones were buried in Turtle's back to feed her — the Mother of all things.

The women fashioned combs from animal teeth and claws. They spent long times combing and caressing each other's hair. They crushed berries and flowers and painted signs on their bodies to honour Mother and the living things who lived with them. They painted on rocks and stones to honour the creatures who taught them. They fixed food together, feeding each other herbs and roots and plants. They lit fires together and cooked the foods that gave them strength and medicine. They laughed together and made language between them. They touched each and in the touching made a new word — love. They touched each other and made a language of touching — passion. They made medicine together. They made magic together.

And on a day when First Woman woke from her sleep, she bled from her body. Sky Woman marvelled at this thing her companion could do because she was born on Turtle's back. Sky Woman built a special place for her companion to retreat at this time, for it was wondrous what her body could do. First Woman went to her bleeding-place and dreamed about her body and the magic it made. And at the end of this time, she emerged laughing and holding out her arms to Sky Woman.

Time went by, long times went by. Sky Woman felt her body changing. Her skin was wrinkling, her hands were not as strong. She could not hunt as she used to. Her eyes were becoming dim, her sight unclear. She walked the earth in this changed body and took longer to climb mountains and swim in the waters. She still enjoyed the touch of First Woman, the laughter and language they shared between them, the dancing, the singing prayers. But her body was changing. Sky Woman whispered to Mother, asking her what these changes meant. Mother whispered back that Sky Woman was aged and soon her body would stop living. Before this event happened, Sky Woman must give her companion instruction. Mother and Sky Woman whispered together the long night through.

When First Woman woke from her sleep, Sky Woman told her of the event that was to happen. "You must cut the heart from this body and bury it in the field by your bleeding-place. Then you must cut this body in small pieces and fling them into the sky. You will do this for me."

And the day came that Sky Woman's body stopped living. First Woman touched her companion's face and promised to carry out her request. She carved the heart from Sky Woman's body and buried it in the open field near her bleeding-place. She put her ear to the ground and heard Sky Woman's voice, "From this place will grow three plants. As long as they grow, you will never want for food or magic. Name these plants corn, beans, and squash. Call them the Three Sisters, for like us, they will never grow apart."

First Woman watched as the green plant burst from the ground, growing stalks which bore ears of beautifully coloured kernels. From beneath the corn rose another plant with small leaves, and it twined around the stalks carrying pods of green and inside each pod were small, white beans. From under the beans came a sprawling vine with large leaves that tumbled and grew and shaded the beans' delicate roots. On this vine were large, green squash that grew and turned orange and yellow. "Three Sisters," First Woman named them.

First Woman cut her companion's body in small pieces and flung them at the sky. The sky turned dark and there, glittering and shining, were bright-coloured stars and a round moon. The moon spoke. "I will come to you everyday when the sun is sleeping. You will make songs and prayers for me. Inside you are growing two beings. They are not like us. They are called Twin Sons. One of these is good and will honour us and our Mother. One of these is not good and will bring things that we have no names for. Teach these beings what we have learned together. Teach them that if the sons do not honour the woman who made them, that will be the end of this earth. Keep well, my beloved First Woman. Eagle is watching out for you. Honour the living things. Be kind to them. Be strong. I am always with you. Remember our Mother. Be kind to her."

First Woman touched her body, feeling the movements inside. She touched the back of Mother and waited for the beings who would change her world.

CAROLYN DUNN

Dying

T HEY SAY SHE IS A SPIRIT, YET SHE IS HUMAN. BORN OF A woman and of a man, but she is not who she says she is at all. You must listen with your open heart and your open mind to understand her. You must look into her eyes just long enough to see who she really is, but if you look long enough you'll find yourself going mad with the possibilities.

The possibilities are endless. The connecting of the universe and the animals and all things in between. She loves, yes, she is a woman, and she understands the meanings and mysteries none of us have been able to understand since long before the time of Removal and we were dispersed and turned into the shapeless things we are now, searching to make up for lost time and love and loss.

I wish I knew how she moves, how she walks, but I know only of hoof marks making tracks in dust, a flash of a dark eye in a headlight, a glimpse of horn and antler in the woods, and when you turn again it's gone. She is there when he touches you, touches you and turns you to fire and light, things you were never meant to be until now. She is there when he looks at you in shame, and you suddenly realize that maybe love is shame after all, and maybe love is not what you thought it was to begin with.

Maybe these are the things she is telling you but you

173

will not listen. She comes to you at 3:33 in the morning, through ancient stars who watched the Old Ones walk the earth long before we were here; up, those stars, taking everything and giving back light and memory and trees that stand tall and wide and she is calling you and you must listen. She tells you of animal spirits you are becoming, but your fear is like hers, and you shut your eyes against what she is telling you because you do not want to believe this about yourself.

You are drawn to danger, to things you should not be drawn to, and she is with you all the way, living in you. They tell you towers are about to fall and you suddenly understand it all because she was with you all along. She was with you through Tennessee, through the Sleeping Woman and with Chief Tahlonteeskee; with you when you rode in silent canoes which sliced through the White River; with you as water turned to blood on the Red River; with you when the Oashita River carried you safely to a new home, one that was not walked to.

She walked behind you in Chicago on hooves of soft white doeskin, but you couldn't hear her as you entered the train and went to the desert valley long before your birth, but you remember because you see it all through their eyes, through her eyes. She is Deer Woman, she is with you now when his eyes turn dark with passion, when his eyes speak of things he cannot tell you but she can. And you know these things, believe them. There is a difference between love, between passion and mercy and true, deep love. But you don't want to know just yet so you ignore what she tells you. You do not listen.

And it's hot, so blazing you think you've become the fire. You're the Eagle now, a dancer with long feathers curved at angles of flight. He tells you to look into the fire but you can't. There's something there. The stones in your hand are those of blood and deep red, and you suddenly understand everything that has come to pass. It's not you anymore, you're not yourself but someone else, the spirits around you have decided it's their voices that want to be heard. It's no longer a dream and shaking, you rise to greet them, all there with words to tell and songs to sing.

It's not your story anymore but hers. She turns those who meet her to madness and you have met her, on the road from there to here. She turns to prostitution or madness, and you have chosen both because they speak of shame and traditions and magic and myth and things you know you are remembering.

And when does she become him? She is him under soft pale moonlight and dark shadows of trees and somewhere in the distance a fire moves like stars. Moon and stars in motion and you can no longer tell the difference between where you end and he begins. His touch is fire, stars, whose fingers spread to the universe of your body, making magic and singing night songs and of things you don't want to believe about yourself, if only you had listened but she was there all along. It's not love you crave, it's him against you, the soft wet taste of his sweat against your skin, his damp hair twisted around your fingers held against his neck and it's not him you love,

175

but the feel of him somehow, if you listen to her, listen long enough you will understand this is not love. It's need. Primal. Raw. Human. Animal.

But then you come to understand the need. Is it need based on what you need or is it need based on animal instincts long held dormant because the woman in you took over when the animal died. And when he holds you in his arms and you're crying like a child, and his heart is there soothing in your ear, you come to understand what love really is, and without her there you become afraid because the instinct is no longer animal. It's comfortable, it's safe. But it's not what you need, she's telling you, because your head turns so easily and your heart turns so bright, bright blood-red stones like the ones in your hand, woven in his hair and your fingers like the Navajo blanket above you, like the Muskogee songs of rattles and tin that move across the wind from the southeasterly way. And once again she becomes you, takes your body, your soul, and you understand the difference between love and passion, between passion and fear, between fear and death, between death and dying.

And you know. You've always known, but you were afraid before. Because there's no longer anyone to protect you. Maybe this is what they were protecting you from, from her, when they brought you to this desert city at the ocean, trying to protect you from the spirits but they were here with you all along, talked to you at night when you were asleep in bed, talked to you through the eyes of children, through the eyes of animals so like your own you knew all along; so now there's no one left to protect you and you are no longer free. The world changes and you look through the eyes of soft velvet tiger eye and rose petals, and wish suddenly, looking down on him, you could see clearly, truly see, and then you realize you have become the deer.

A little bit dies each time, with each breath, but your skin cracks and falls away, shining and becomes dust to the earth, the red wet with our blood and the salt from our tears, and you fall, a piece of you falls, and no longer will he look at you with shame because you have him, taken him into your body, where he tries to escape and will not because he has entered you, and this time he will not leave. This time, you have taken him in and he is lost, there are no divisions between your boundary and his, like a map of virgin territory, and you have reclaimed it, and with your power, erased those red lines etched with your ancestors' blood and you look at him with eyes that have no fear, no loss, no memory, eyes of seven stars who sing of the Old Ones and we have become reborn.

I opened my eyes against the soft pale light which crept into the bedroom behind tiny metal shades and slits of aluminum. I could smell the scent of wet earth and wet sky, sense the coldness that permeated the room, but under three comforters and an electric blanket, I was quite warm. There was movement next to me, around me, and I glanced down at the shiny, long dark hair of my son, nestled between the warmth of my body, under the warmth of the three quilts and one electric blanket, and Stephen's long, tall frame stretched from one end of the bed to the other. I watched as my son turned in his sleep, his shiny, dark head barely peeping out from the blankets.

Reluctantly, I rose from our bed. The floor was cold, with an iciness that penetrated to the bone. This is what winter is like here behind the Redwood Curtain, the low rumbling in my lungs reminding me that my chronic bronchitis was about to burst to the surface, revived by our latest storm.

I tiptoed across the floor, careful not to wake the boys. My son, John Tahlonteeskee Emmanuel, Tahlon, one half of a whole that would never be part of me again. His father, Wesley Harjo, the Cree half-blood whose green eyes spoke of shame and despair every waking and sleeping moment; and Tahlon's twin Thomas Harjo Emmanuel, my grey-eyed, blond-headed, fragile, and fresh faced little boy whose spirit was not of this world, who still once in a while looked at me through Tahlon's dark old soul-eyes, eyes that were not of my world but one that had long since passed.

The fire from the stove had gone out. Shivering, I entered the cold living room, but the walls still held some remembrance of warmth and I was relieved. I leaned down and put a dry cedar log into the stove and lit a new fire. I turned from the stove and moved into the kitchen, my feet silently padding across the hardwood floor. The coffee was made, so black no light can shine through, and I poured myself half a cup and drowned the rest in milk, turning the mixture a nice shade of skin colour.

Sunlight filled the room. Normally, I am not one to rise with the sun, long having abandoned that tradition because of my natural reticence toward anything before 7:30 a.m. But I had dreamt the night before, of Salmon Creek, of a flash beating softly in my ear, of Thomas's clear, grey eyes, of a tiny hand touching my face, and of Paul Burns moving, changing, trying to get out of his body and rise up toward the clear, starless vacuum of the night.

The trees outside shone in sunlight, green needles reflecting deep shades of shiny newness and brown bark, deep, wet, alive. Roots spread below the ground, rising toward the sun and spreading across the dark earth, covered in red and brown dead leaves blown free from last night's deep, fast winds. There's something about the brightness of the dark, wet trees, something that crosses the fine line between darkness and light, a space of earth that when wet, gives off light and newness of life that can overcome any darkness, even that of a black clouded sky and gusts of violent wind, and the death of a brother. Death of a son.

Nothing about Paul surprised me anymore. There was too much history behind us, too many summers up in the hills beyond Salmon Creek and too many years etched in rock and wood all along the highway, flowers marking graves. Even when he brought that baby back from Gallup and moved in with Annalee when we all lived in the city and expected her to understand, expected all of us to understand. Not even when he would stay for weeks and weeks without a word to anyone, then suddenly appear along the highway somewhere, his thumb standing straight up in a salute to heaven, moving up and down with each step as if he was trying to fly. Not even when his lips touched mine on the mountain, sliding his body against mine and bringing me to what my madness — and my wisdom — were about, sending me home to Wesley and the Muskogee blood that flowed between us. But this — his latest disappearance — this surprised me.

I knew what it was about. I'd seen him last five months earlier, on his way to Gallup and needing a ride to Garberville. Yes, he still moved and danced his steps, yes he was still his usual self, quiet, self-reliant, watching. But it was his eyes, behind his glasses, that told another story. "Grandpa saw the fires," he'd told me long ago, "now I smell 'em behind every tree, every rock, every road kill. They're with me, the spirits, you know." He was lost to us. And it was forever. He leaned into the car, smiled, and slumped his shoulder so his backpack slid down his arm to his neck. "Bye, Carlisle," he'd said with a smile. "Bye."

Bye, I whispered now, on the cold linoleum floor of my kitchen, the grey rapidly changing to blue sky hovering above my window. Bye.

What can I say about Paul that would possibly make

me understand him any better? I loved him once, loved him so fiercely and with such promise that the wind got knocked out of me. He was loved by all of us, by me, even by Wesley, by his brother, my Stephen, and of course by Annalee. But none of us could ever prepare ourselves for the shock of his disappearance, which we all knew was his death. If I could look at the underlying current that ran between us, it was Paul. But none of us understood him, all of us loved him, and none of us could have saved him. He would not be saved.

Bye, I whispered again, though no one heard.

Thomas Harjo Emmanuel. Thomas, eyes wide open and the colour of that grey sky. Thomas, with a purpose already served, his breath my breath, my heart his heart. They were twins. Twin sons. Just like Wild Boy and Corn Brother, Wild Boy formed from his mother's thick dark blood and spirit essence; Corn Brother from the earth and sky, Corn Mother and Kanati. Corn Mother spilt her own blood to the earth to form them. And the spirits, they are not mine to keep, so they drift to the next one who needs them, maybe more than I ever did. Dine spirits. Muskogee spirits. Like the wind.

A laughing Navajo boy, maybe once laughing, maybe not ever. I don't think Paul ever laughed much. Come to think of it, I don't think I ever heard him laugh at all. I'd seen his boy smile, like it had always been between us. But the laughter, the sound of it, would've changed the silence between us, silence that made his deliverance a little more tolerable.

The morning sends pictures of tolerance my way. The sky at dawn, the way the world turns that reddish shade of gold, showering sprays of light across everything beneath the sunrise. It warms me, fills me with light, that tolerance, tolerance of my child's eyes in heaven, tolerance of my grandmother's voice in the sky, tolerance of Wesley's leaving, tolerance of Annalees's deteriorating health, tolerance of the aloneness and desperation, tolerance of Paul's love, tolerance of the dying. There are seasons that are a part of us and at every turn one thing must come to an end.

I look at endings. Dyings. Whispers on the dark line of morning against the sand and water horizon. I have weathered many more endings than beginnings. The end of my sister Kim, who left us because she could no longer tolerate the world. The body washes in ash, flying on the wind. My father Johnny, who, because he could not protect Kim from herself, allowed his heart to break and shatter like thousands of tiny glass beads turned to shards of crimson tearing at the fabric of my own world. My own world: the message from either side: "too black to be Indian, too Indian to be black," spoke louder than any words they would have said. My love for Wesley — whose green eyes betrayed him — the father of my twins, the one who left me before the leaving was done; Paul, who could have been the father of my twins, the other father, whose eyes spoke of shame and despair whenever he looked at me, who taught me the madness to begin with, until I looked down and saw my own hooves;

Annalee's burning candles and charges of hope giving
her strength and light and love healing her dying; my
Thomas, the twin, who left me on a cold starlit morning,
his dark grey eyes and face so angelic, so sweet, so impas-
sioned in his leaving me; and now Stephen, my rock, the
one who led me to the living by needing me for the
strength through my dead. Sharon Burch sings, "I'm in
love with a Navajo boy" and I'm drawn by him. I cover
his walls, his scenery becomes my flesh. And in the dying
the flesh flakes fall away and become the living. We are
needful of these things, wish and pray for them but they
only remain constant and aloof. And I'm reminded by
Stephen's eyes, by the steady way in which he plants
himself in the soil of my earth, my garden and I am
blessed by his presence, by the beauty that is him.

So in the dying I live — in the wasteland the hazards
of my life begin anew. I have died a thousand times not
to be reborn but to live. And I survive. I tell the stories of
us, so that we can learn. Deer Woman, the awi spirit,
came to me once a long time ago, living in Paul, until by
his loving me, entered my body and I met her. But I
looked down. I saw my own hooves and understood the
magic, understood the lines etched into my blood by my
Muskogee ancestors. But Paul, the Dine spirit, could
never understand and he didn't see her feet. They say
Deer Woman turns those she meets to madness, illness, or
death if they do not understand her power. And to understand her power is to understand the spirit nature and
woman she is. To understand that power, they say, you

must look to her feet and see the hooves. Then you can truly understand that she is a woman, and by her hooves she is a deer.

My madness saved me; Paul's put him into the land of the dead. I tell the stories so we can all be returned to that place in the morning where I stand and from the soft place of the linoleum, cold to the touch, I regain my senses and tolerate even the rising sun.

I am free, standing at the morning. And Tahlon comes in, the voice of eagles and stars, and sings to me:

"Mama."

I turn, Tahlon stands in the doorway, rubbing his eyes with the backs of both fists. I am smiling. "Hey there my sonny son-son," I hold out my arms.

John Tahlonteeskee Emmanuel walks across the floor, bold, brave and brash, crawls up my legs and to my lap, moves inside the circle my arms hold for him, pushing the old purple afghan under his chin. The window turns reflections of grey, yellow, then grey again, and I can see the colour of my son's eyes in the sky as his twin, my son, lies dreaming, wrapped in the circle of my grandmother's blanket and my arms.

Ruth Huntsinger

The Story of the People

FAR TO THE NORTH, WHERE WINTERS STRETCHED LONG, cold hands to catch the hunters who travelled too far from their camp, there dwelled a tribe of the people.

One day two strangers who said that they were also members of the people, but of a different tribe, came to the lodges of the far north people. The travellers said that they wished to bring their people to the northern lodges to live for the remainder of the winter as they were hungry and had much need for food and robes.

The Chief agreed to call a council of the elders so the strangers might come before them. As the elders and the guests entered the council lodge, an old woman watched. When she saw that the strangers did not lay away their weapons before entering the lodge, she became very angry that the tribe's hospitality had been so defiled and so she stayed on the outside to watch and listen.

After the men had smoked the pipe together, the strangers told of their trouble and asked if they might bring their people to the far north camp. Now, the chiefs were solely troubled because the people did not like to refuse another request; it was their way to share whatever they had with all. But the elders realized that if they let the other tribe move in with them, that all might go hungry. Perhaps some of their own old people or children

185

might even die for they had to rely on the food that they had gathered and stored for the winter months.

An old chief admired a knife that one of the strangers was wearing. The man took the knife from its sheath and ran his fingers over the blade, agreeing that it was a very good knife. Then he plunged it into a piece of meat and began to eat.

The woman on the outside saw that and uttered under her breath for now she knew why she had stayed. She ran to tell the other women what she had seen and heard.

The chief told the guests that the council must consider the matter and they would have an answer the next morning.

When the strangers left the lodge, a large crowd of women followed them to the outskirts of the camp. Then with a screech the women tore the strangers' robes from them, and the whiteness of their skin gleamed so that all could see.

The woman had thought that they were not one of them when they did not set aside their weapons before entering the lodge, but she knew they were not when it was apparent they had come only to take and not to give; for all the people gave as a gift what was admired by another.

JAN BOURDEAU (WABOOSE)

The Buckskin Jacket

> "Let us treat each other with respect, for
> we are all human beings. Do not judge, by the
> colour of the skin, where one may live,
> or the language one may speak."

> "Let us live in harmony on this Earth."

> "Let us not speak ugly words to one another."
> "Let us not fight with one another."

> "Instead we must combine our efforts and energies,
> together, and direct them at saving our precious
> environment...our Earth."

> "Let us not destroy Nature and Mankind too."

"HEY, NO WAY I'M SITTING BESIDE HER."
He stood eyeing her; his face had that ugly look she had seen many times before.

Patsy sighed. A deep heavy breath came from her. It wasn't the first time she had heard a remark like that.

But today it was going to be different. At least that's what she had promised herself.

High school. She was 13 and starting high school. It was to be a new start for her. No one would know her. No one would know she lived on the "other side of the river."

187

Not like in public school. The kids there were mean. They said hurtful things. Patsy remembered how the kids would run away from her and her sister, screaming, "Red Injuns. Red Injuns. Here come the Red Injuns." Then they would make strange "whooping sounds" by beating their hands on their lips as they ran.

Patsy thought about the boy in grade six, who had that "ugly" look on his face. She remembered him standing, pointing at her and talking loudly. He boasted, "My dad says, Indians are good for nothing — can't even take care of themselves. It's a good thing we keep them on the other side of the river."

Patsy didn't like public school. She didn't like the kids and she didn't like living "on the other side of the river." She would wonder if it was the way they dressed that made the kids make fun of them.

Their clothes were second-hand, but pressed and clean. Mother would braid their hair using strings of leather woven through the braiding. On their feet they wore moccasins that Nokomis, her grandmother, had made.

Patsy and her sister, who was a year and a bit younger never spoke in their native tongue at school. Patsy felt humiliated and hurt when she was teased and taunted. She would be silent. If only she could be invisible.

Her sister would just get angry, but she would never show her anger to the other kids. She would stand there, face her taunters and say, "All of you and your silly

name-calling make me laugh. You just make me laugh."
And then a loud burst of strange laughter would come
from her throat.

Some days Patsy would hear her sister's strange
laughter from across the school yard and know what was
going on.

But that was public school. Patsy was older now.
The new students would be older, too. They would be
different. They would not treat her that way. Besides, no
one knew her. No one knew she lived "on the other side
of the river." No one knew she was Indian.

When she dressed for school that morning she did
not put on the beaded hair clips, that her mother had
made. She deliberately avoided braiding her long, dark
hair and she did not let it hang long and straight down
her back. In fact, with great trouble the night before, she
had curled it.

She did not wear the beaded buckskin jacket,
Mishomis, her grandfather had proudly given her for
graduating. Her outer skin, he called it.

She made sure her mother did not see her leave
without it this morning. She did not want to tell her why
she couldn't wear it today.

But it had not made any difference. Because there he
stood, with that "ugly" look on his face. Pointing at her.

"I said I'm not sitting beside a squaw so you'd better
move."

Patsy meekly looked around, avoiding everyone's
eyes. There were no other desks in the classroom. There

was no where else to sit. Her heart sank. She could feel all eyes on her. The burning in her cheeks was unbearable. Her long ridiculous looking curls fell across her face, hiding it.

Her skin was not the colour of her sister's. Patsy's skin was lighter. Much lighter. And Patsy's eyes were deep brown, not shining black like her sister's.

She had looked at herself for a long time in the mirror before she left this morning.

"No one will know. No one will know," she had told herself.

But she was wrong!

"Well, you're a squaw aren't you?" the ugly face demanded.

Patsy looked up from staring at the finger nail polish she'd put on the night before. Why had she chosen the colour white?

"Hey, are you deaf too? What is it with you? Don't you understand English? Or maybe you just speak squaw language?"

He laughed very loudly. It sounded like a roar in her ears.

"I said you're an Indian, aren't you?"

"No." Patsy heard a quiet shy voice. It had come from her. Suddenly she felt angry. Angry at the voice of denial. The room was silent. Then he spoke again.

"Well, pardon me. A case of mistaken identity," he sneered.

"But you look like you could be."

"Well, I'm not. I'm not." She denied it again.

"Then who cares where you sit." He shrugged his shoulders and sat down beside her, careful not to sit too close at the double desk, lest he touch her.

She could feel his body heat and hear his breathing. She hated being this close to him. She hated being in this class. She wondered if she should hate him.

Before her Mishomis died, he had told her, "Do not hate. It is a destructive thing. It will destroy who you are. From Mother Earth come many things. The people, the trees, the animals, the birds — they are all different, but yet, we are all the same. To hate would be to hate yourself. Don't ever do that. Don't ever deny who you are."

Patsy felt sick. She had betrayed Mishomis and she had betrayed herself.

Why wasn't she born with the dark skin of her sister? There would be no chance of denying it then. She would be Native for all the world to see. There would be no doubt.

Patsy could feel the "ugly face" staring at her. He was about to say something, when the teacher walked in. She was relieved.

"Good morning new students. Welcome to Chauncellor High. I'm glad you have found your seating arrangements for the year. The student beside you will be your project partner."

Patsy heard a loud groan. Beside her, he had slid down half way under the desk. She winced in silence.

"Go ahead, introduce yourselves to your partner."

The teacher insisted.

The ugly face turned. He spoke.

"Look, I'm Bill. I live on the upper part of town — away from the river. And you already know I don't like Indians. I think they are bums. My dad does, too. There, that's all you need to know. Don't bother telling me about yourself. You already told me all I needed to know. So we're project partners. Big Deal!"

Patsy swallowed, but her mouth was dry. Her tongue stuck to the roof of it. She could feel her heart echoing within her body. She avoided his piercing blue eyes.

"Tell him, tell him who you are," the angry voice pleaded from inside.

Again the teacher spoke.

"This class is dismissed. Tomorrow will be a longer day." Patsy wondered how tomorrow could possibly be any longer than this. She slowly gathered her books, keeping her head down, avoiding any eyes looking at her. But she could feel them. The boy with the ugly look was moving away from the desk, heading towards the open door, smirking and strutting with every step.

Suddenly, as he moved away, Patsy heard him say.

"Look what we have here — a squaw, a real live squaw, right from the other side of the river, the Indian reserve slums. That's what my dad calls it." He bellowed while she cringed. Was he doing it to her again? She looked up.

By the door stood a young girl with long raven-coloured hair. It was braided and held by two beaded hair clips. Her eyes were the colour of the night. Her skin was the colour of the earth. She stood proud and tall, waiting by the classroom door.

Patsy was suddenly filled with guilt and pride at the same time. Again she heard a voice coming from her throat.

"She is my sister."

Her voice sounded strong and proud. "And I am your project partner. And you...make me laugh." A loud burst of strange laughter came from her. A laughter she had heard many times before.

He turned and scowled at her. She looked back at him. Straight at him. He did not look "ugly" to her anymore. She felt sadness for him. He did not speak again. He brushed by her in his haste to leave, trying to flee the stares from the other students. And he was gone.

Patsy's sister smiled at her. She spoke in their native tongue. In Ojibway, she said. "My laughing sister, here is your buckskin. Mother said you had forgotten it this morning. Your outer skin, as Mishomis would say. She said it could get very cold without it."

"Yeah, I know — but I have it now." Patsy reached for her beaded buckskin jacket and put it on.

"Meegwetch." She hugged her sister.

SHIRLEY BEAR

Diamonds of the Forest

> Seven went up the holy mountain.
> Will the Creator honour them with a sign?
> Seven unholy maidens,
> Seven unvirginly ones,
> Huffing and climbing
> To the beat of raindrops.
> "Diamonds of the forest," she said.

THIS IS NOT WHAT I INTENDED TO DO THIS EVENING. I just wonder if it's slightly better than sticking around and listening to depressing stories of the harsh realities of so many different women. What a climb! It's wet and slippery and downright dangerous for a person my age. Downright dangerous? Emily and her friend Christine seem so unsure; they may be questioning the validity of our ascension of this mountain.

Earlier we had come up here and heard the beautiful story of the holy persons who have fasted for four to seven days. Long time fasting intrigues me because of my own quests.

It's an unusually humid night for October. The warmth and the dampness combined feel like a very warm sweat. Raindrops have attached themselves to firs and cedars like little crystal marbles. The setting sun hazes through the rain clouds and gives these woods an ethereal glow and sparkle.

Pokjinsquas, assuming an authoritative stance, continues her narrative:

> She fasted for four days,
> Then for seven, each time
> Not wanting to return.
> She never told anyone why.
> She never shared what she learned.
> Then she never returned.
> No one has ever seen her.
> The years went by
> And one day a prophet foretold
> The birth of a special teacher,
> A young man.
> He had heard the stories of the mountain,
> And the fast and the dreams.
> He wanted more than the stories.
> He wanted the dreams.

This sounds too much like a Bible story. I wonder how many of our stories contain stories told to us by the religious, who managed to convince us of their truths. I wonder how many of these stories are their old stories — and not ours.

I'm glad that some of the women gathered dry twigs on the way up the mountain, for now our fire is starting to warm us. This weekend retreat is just what I needed to slow my pace in the world as we know it today. One

positive aspect is the bringing together of this many
women from the four directions of this turtle island.

Life is pretty hectic in my job at the reserve band
office. We spend an inordinate amount of time battling
with the government for survival dollars. Just last week
we had to turn away about eighty families who are on
social assistance because our chief would not agree to
barter away certain rights in exchange for the release of
the quarterly funds, already two weeks overdue. It is not
uncommon for government bureaucrats to hold back
funds for insignificant reasons, in their efforts to force
assimilation of the original people of this turtle island.
What is unfortunate is the subtle use of blackmail
through the social programs. Anyway, we were dis-
mayed at the action of the bureaucrats because we know
that for the majority of these families on social assistance
these funds mean the next meal on the table.

Marlene, a young mother of five children, felt she
would have to turn to prostitution again to earn the
money needed to feed her children, until the situation
could be straightened out. When I approached her with
some money, she was adamant in her refusal, proclaim-
ing that she would not accept charity and that she already
owed too much to too many people.

Up here on the mountain, with the spirits of centuries surrounding us, the band offices seem as many centuries away.

He saw many visions
And learned many lessons.
He fasted and dreamed for many years.
He returned to his family many times.
Then one day the eagle came.
"Climb on my back!" the eagle ordered.
He flew far, and learned many things.
He learned about fire.
He learned about water.
He learned about the earth and the sky.
He learned as his mind burned
An imprint of his body
Into the stone, into the mountain.
And he came back.

In the years that followed
He taught the people
All the rituals he knew,
All the ceremonies.
About the pipe, the drum
And the sacred sweat.
About the sage, cedar, and sweetgrass.

Emily and Christine have heard the story many
times before, but they stand quietly, listening. There's a
soft hum like a woman's lullaby to her tired baby. It is
soothing, melodious. I begin to wonder if Pokjinsquas, in
her magical way, has also managed to hum as she speaks.
I strain to hear but it is a hum that seems to fill the air

197

without being overpowering. I glance around at the other women.

Shelley has her eyes closed and I can't tell if she also hears the humming. If anyone is likely to tune into the other world, I guess it would be her, being a musician.

Frances, in her unconventional attire, also has her eyes closed and is swaying slightly. Her face looks as though it were lit up from inside. She looks so...un-Frances.

Frances is a struggling writer. Her writing deals with the injustices of the world, both on the national scale and within the community. She will be a great writer because of the questioning forces within her. Her youth will allow her access to experiences that we can only recount through a biased memory.

Marilyn stands beside me and I can't see her clearly but I can feel her fidgeting; she seems very uncomfortable. She is certainly not dressed for a mountain hike. She had to borrow walking shoes before we started the climb and her fashionable Bay Street dress seems out of place here on the mountain in a soft rain. Maybe that's the reason she's so uncomfortable. It's getting chilly so I add twigs to the fire.

> Seven women heard the story
> Of the woman who never came back.
> Seven women heard the story
> Of the man who learned and taught
> Until he was very old.

Seven women burned tobacco
And sang and waited.
Then she came.
Her long white hair flowed past her feet
As she knelt, making her offering to the Creator.
She offered incense of sage and sweetgrass
In thanksgiving for all that had been,
For all that was to come,
And for all that was to be.
She made her offerings and asked
That her dreams be shared
With her descendants:
Her dreams of the coming of the "Whenooj,"
Hairy-faced men in long robes,
Who would steal the spirit of the people.
Of the suffering and unspeakable losses:
Loss of spirit power,
Loss of land,
Loss of language,
Loss of the original way of life.
These were her original words.

Seven women on the Mount of Dreams.
Four seeing the emergence of the original story:
One woman from the East,
One woman from the South,
One woman from the West,
One woman from the North.
The storyteller and a woman from the centre

Heard, saw and always knew
That the dreamer would someday return.
From the four directions
The women had come
And to the four directions
They would return
With the original story.

As I flew home, relaxing in a comfortable cushioned seat on a huge aircraft, my mind pondered the events of the weekend. How insignificant all the systemized workshops appeared now. All I seemed to remember was the woman with her long white hair flowing, the humming of her song, a healing that was meant for all of the women who attended the gathering.

I realized that I would return to the band office and continue the battle with the government for a more just application of programs within the aboriginal community. I knew also that this was not the answer.

As the vision returns to me, I also know what I really have to do.

ANITA ENDREZZE

There was a Yaqui Woman

H E LEANED AGAINST THE REFRIGERATOR, WATCHING me as I did the dishes. I was doing them very carefully, not wanting to give him my full attention. I soaped a glass, rinsed it under running water, turning it until the glass squeaked clean against my fingertips. Then I picked up the damp dish towel and wiped the glass slowly. I looked out the window. Even though it was mid-morning, it was dark out. Rain blew in gusts, spattering the window. I could barely make out the blurry shapes of red and yellow tulips, their petals turned inside out by the wind.

"So," he said, but it was really a question. I kept wiping the glass, seeing him out of the corner of my eye.

Things hadn't been going very well between us lately. I could sense his body tight with anger. That anger was like a creature with sharp, snapping teeth. I shivered. Was this creature my husband? Or was it created by him — a thing full of bitter hungers? I didn't know him anymore.

Finally, I put down the glass and towel. I faced him, silent, waiting.

He spoke again, irritated."So? So?"

"What?"

"Jeez." He ran his fingers through his hair, his knuckles looking like pure bones, fleshless, but gouged with teeth marks. I could feel eyes all around us. "Jeez," he said again.

I relented. I knew what he was talking about, but I didn't want to make it too easy for him. He could always out-argue me, so I had ways to get back at him. I have my own weapons, like little arrows made of the shiftiest sand, but with barbs that got under his skin.

"Okay," I said. "I don't want to go."

Bob stared at me. "I'm trying to understand, Lori. Really I am."

I didn't want to go to his family's Easter dinner. But it was hard for me to explain why. I don't have a lot of fancy words. I just finished my GED. Boy, it was hard. That math test scared me to death. I couldn't keep all those numbers in my mind. They just didn't stand still. Like rain drops sizzling on a hot stone.

So I don't have much education, although I plan on attending the community college next fall. I know I don't know that much, but I know what I feel. I just can't say it very well.

I could hear teeth gnashing and looked up sharply at my husband, but his mouth was still, set in a grim line. He was waiting for my explanation.

I sighed and crossed my arms. This was an old argument between us.

"You know. It's your parents. I'm tired of them calling me That Little Indian Girl." I stopped, wondering if I should go on.

He walked over to the sink, took the glass I had just

dried, and filled it up with water. I watched him drink, aware that I no longer liked seeing his adam's apple bobbing up and down. His strong throat muscles constricting the air and water disgusted me. I don't know what's wrong with me anymore.

"We've been married a long time, Lori. Why all the fuss now? Just forget what they say. That's their generation. They don't know any better and they're not going to change."

"It bothers me," I replied. And in an attempt to be more forceful, I added, "A lot."

He shook his head. It bothered me that my being bothered didn't bother him. It was obvious that he didn't see me as I saw myself. But for years I've only seen myself through his eyes, so maybe I'm not sure of what there is of me to see.

"I'm confused." I didn't mean to say this out loud. A voice inside of me whispered: *Never admit your weakness to your enemy.* I was filled with an aching sadness. Was this man, whom I had once loved, an enemy? I remember when his touch sent delicious pains racing through my body. Now, I didn't know what I felt. This was all my fault; my problem. I'm changing.

As I've gotten older, I seemed to listen more to the old Indian ways. It was as if life was a whirlpool. I was being drawn in, pulled into the centre of the universe by strong brown hands with gentle touches.

Bob laughed sourly. "No shit," he said. " *You're* confused? I'm confused. I don't know what the hell you want. What's so bad about being called an Indian girl? What are you, a monkey?"

I was quiet. I could see the fangs in the corners of the room. Bob says my imagination is always working overtime.

It wasn't what was said so much, but how his parents said it. And what wasn't said. Like my name. They never called me by my name, not after all these years. I was just "That Little Indian Girl." I am 26 years old.

I took the creature by the tail. "It's more than that."

"Like what?"

"The last time we got together, your father told Annie that if she didn't behave, he'd sell her to the wild Indians."

Anne is our oldest daughter. She is seven going on 80. She acts like a wise grandmother, but she's also a kid and likes to play. She had been squealing and shrieking that time. All the kids had been getting too wound up.

My husband straightened up. He's a tall, big man. I cranked my neck back to look at him. "I agree," he said, "that's not a good thing to say, but it's just an expression. It doesn't mean anything."

"Yes, it does!" I felt myself shaking slightly. I had talked to Anne afterward. She'd been upset. She'd wanted to know why Gramps had said that and I didn't have an answer for her. I wanted to teach her about being Indian, but I didn't want her to experience racism and ignorance.

My husband countered my thoughts. "Lori, you can't

shelter the girls from reality."

"They're so young," I whispered. I remember how Annie had asked me why Whites hated Indians. I told her that most Whites don't hate Indians. "Well," she had told me, "I hate them!" I sighed and, holding her hand, I told her she shouldn't hate. "After all," I said, "you'd only be hating part of yourself. You're White and Indian."

She asked me to tell Gramps not to say such bad things. But I hadn't done anything. I didn't want to face his parents. I was afraid. Maybe that too much rage would pour out. Or maybe I was just too weak in character.

Bob walked back to the refrigerator. He was fiddling with the magnets that held up the girls' drawings. When he spoke, he spoke as if he was trying to get a lesson across to a slow learner.

"Well, Lori, if what my parents say bothers you so much, why don't you tell them?"

I shook my head quickly. It seemed like the obvious thing to do, but I just couldn't. I felt weary. I could sense the creature's knife-like teeth clicking all around me. Bob should talk to them; they were *his* parents.

Besides, I just didn't have the words. How could I explain that I didn't want Annie or Nina to grow up gaining their identity from a constant fight against life? I wanted their sense of themselves to come from a goodness from within. Maybe I was naive. I don't know. I was their mother. I should be standing up for them. I should be a warrior-woman.

My husband had an army of teeth around him. "So, that's it, huh? You won't go to the Easter dinner because you don't like my parents."

He always says things that are partly true, yet not quite enough for me to agree with. But to explain seems to take too much energy. I deflected his shot.

"Well," I said, "You know I'm not a Christian."

He exploded in the fierce whispers parents use when they are arguing within earshot of their children. "Jeez, what does that have to do with it? It's a family tradition, for chrissakes! You are always going on and on about family and tradition!"

He paused, wiping his hands on his jeans." And another thing, I'm sick and tired of you going on about being Indian."

I widened my eyes. "But I am!"

He snorted. "Some Indian you are. You can't speak your own tribe's language, you don't live in a teepee ..."

I muttered, "Yaquis never lived in teepees..." But he didn't hear me.

"You live in a real nice house..."

I rolled my eyes up. It was a five-room tract house, built in 1949 to house workers from the Kaiser aluminum plant. It had no insulation, the concrete porch was cracked, and the kitchen was so tiny that I kept some of my seldom-used pans under our bed.

"You have your own car... "

I stared at him. It was a big white chevy that I called Moby Dick. There were mice in the trunk and dashboard.

Whenever I turned on the heater, bits of fluff from their nest puffed out. The floor mat under my feet covered a piece of cardboard. Under the cardboard was nothing but open road. It had rusted out completely.

"You watch TV, you wear lipstick, you couldn't kill a deer for food if your life depended on it. You'd think it was Bambi!" He laughed at me. "Some Indian! I'll tell you what, Lori, you're an Indian alright, a book Indian, but you're no Yaqui."

I had to think about that for a while. Was he right? Sure, I didn't know my tribe's language. Neither did my father and he was a full-blood. Lots of Indians were forced to speak English. That was not their disgrace. No, it was to their credit that they still believed in themselves; that they still passed on their stories.

The stories were my lifeline to the past. They defined my awareness. While shaping the words to my children as I told them the old stories, the words shaped me.

Bob and I were facing each other. There were only a few feet between us, yet, such a great distance.

"And another thing," he said, "you never want sex anymore."

Now, even the snapping teeth were silent. I held my breath. How did we get to this? What could I say?

Then Annie walked in. She'd been watching cartoons on TV. She was singing.

"We're tiny, we're tooney, we're all a little looney."

She stopped, sensing the other creatures and their eyes. I could see her looking at me and her father. I think she was trying to see if the creatures' eyes were our eyes or if we were still her parents.

"Are you hungry?" I asked. Anything to fill that silence, that emptiness.

She shook her head. "Come and watch TV with us. Please? *Both* of you."

The peacemaker.

"Later, honey," said her father. "We're busy right now."

Her eyes flickered uneasily and then she asked for a glass of water.

My husband gave her the glass he'd been drinking out of. I was afraid it was full of anger. I took it from him and rinsed it out carefully. I could feel his body stiffening. Now I had insulted him. He didn't say anything. I filled the glass with cold water and gave it to Annie. She left.

The room seemed airless. I avoided his last question by repeating that I didn't want to go to that dinner.

He squared his shoulders. "So what the hell do you want?"

I could feel the teeth gnawing at my stomach. How could I make him understand that I wasn't sure myself? I knew I wanted to be stronger. For my daughters and for myself. I wanted to be a strong, mixed-blood woman. I wasn't sure how. And then I remembered a story about my Yaqui great-grandmother.

I faced my husband. I would tell him this story. I didn't need words to explain. The old words would work.

I began, "There was this Yaqui woman... "

"Oh, Jeez," he groaned. "You always do that!"

"What?"

"You know what. I ask you to tell me how you feel, what you think, and you go off on some Indian story that doesn't have a point to it."

"No, I don't."

"Yes, you do."

"They all have points." You just don't get it, I said gloomily to myself.

"Besides, what does some old story have to do with now?"

"What's now?" I asked. Another of my weapons. Answer a question with a question. Kind of a two-headed arrow.

"Jeez Luuuueeezzz!" he turned around in a half-circle, like he was dancing. "I don't want some meta-physical crap about time again! Who the shit cares! Grow up, Lori! All I want to know is about the fuckin' Easter dinner and what the hell's gonna happen to us!"

There was a small second of silence before the phone rang. His words had shattered the shadows. The crea-tures were clearer. They looked like larvae with dozens of fingers groping out of their thick bodies and on each finger, each tooth. They wiggled on the kitchen floor, in the air, and squirmed around my ankles. They were chalk white with muddy bands of adobe red encircling their bodies. They had no faces, just feral eyes, and teeth. I must be crazy to see such things.

Bob answered the phone on the third ring. It was his partner, Richard Beacon, from work. My husband turned to face the phone on the wall and I could see the back of his neck. Where the skin creased, it was reddish, but when he moved his head, the skin crackled white.

I was going to tell him about my great-grandmother, Empimenia.

Her husband had been murdered by robbers. He had a pack train; he was a trader, you see. And he'd take his mules and goods from village to village all along the coast of northwestern Mexico. But then some Mexicans, dressed as Indians, killed him. They took everything.

My great-grandmother was a tiny woman. She wasn't even five feet tall. But she went to the law there and with two huge pistols on her hips, she told the sheriff, "Find out who killed my husband and bring them to justice. Or you will be the next to die."

That was the story. Now my husband would say, "So? So? So, what happened? Did the sheriff catch the murderers?"

I don't know. I don't think that's the point. The story was passed down from mother to daughter, to show that a woman can have courage.

It was the courage of direct confrontation, something I wasn't very good at. Bob was right. I should grow up.

I felt strength entering me. I had carried my daughters inside of me, letting them dream their way into being. My womb had been a circle, my heart the first drum beat they'd heard. I must be strong so that they will become strong women and mothers.

My husband hung up the phone. I didn't hate him. He wasn't the enemy. He wasn't bad. We were just too different.

There was a deep pain in his face as he looked at me. His eyes were bewildered, angry, hurt.

"I try to tell you things," I said, softly, "but in my own way."

His shoulders sagged. "I'm just so fuckin' tired of this crap."

I didn't know what to say. I could hear my grandmothers' voices singing their high-pitched songs. The teethed creatures slithered away from them as the women danced.

My husband straightened up. "Well, I'm taking the girls to that damn dinner. You can just stay home."

"No!" I couldn't believe he'd do that!

He stared at me. "Look, Lori. They're my kids, too. And they have the right to learn *my* heritage, *my* religion! Isn't this America? Huh? Aren't we supposed to be Americans first? What you want to teach them is some kind of racist crap about being Indian and I'd like them to know about their White blood, which is pretty damn good. I don't want them to be ashamed of being White, Lori. You've turned into some kind of stranger to me. I don't like your racist attitude."

I was shocked.

He went on. "So I'm taking them to the dinner."

He crossed his arms and stared at me.

"No..." I wanted to argue with him about everything he had said. He had the wrong idea.

"No?" His head reared back in mock shock. He was laughing at me, in his bitter need to win.

"No." I didn't say the word very often in my life. It felt like a piece of sharp obsidian but it became smoother the more I said it.

"And another thing," he said, jabbing his fingers in the air for emphasis. He was shouting his weapons faster than I could shield myself. Then I knew we were fighting on unequal terms: I had arrows, he had an uzi. "You need to see a counsellor. Get over this thing."

"What thing? What?"

"Or get a job."

"I thought I had a job, caring for our daughters. And I'm going to school soon."

"I mean a real job. With money coming in. Get out of the house. Have a life."

I was trembling. His words didn't make any sense; he had too many teeth in his mouth. His tongue was full of teeth, big, flat, shingle-teeth.

He laughed. "You don't know anything about the real world, Lori. You want to be an artist. Ha! You'd better take classes in typing or something. I can't afford to pay for you to go to school to study painting, for chrissakes!"

I was wordless again, my whole body leaning towards the whirlpool, a drumming sound beginning in my toes. I could see the grandmothers twirling and dancing and grinning. They liked a good fight.

"So," my husband said, his hands on his hips, "for the last time tell me what you *do* want." He was being Mr. Fair-minded himself.

There was a silence so deep that I could hear the crunching sounds of the creatures as they consumed themselves.

Alright, I thought. Now was the time for me to make my decision about my life. The grandmothers waved to me, stomping their feet like impatient horses. Well, I'd have to tell him *my* way, whether he liked it or not. I had remembered a story.

I began with deep breath. "There was a Yaqui woman... "

"Jeez, jeez, jeez!" He grabbed his hair and moaned. "I thought I told you..."

"Wait. Let me tell you just this one story. Please! Listen."

He sighed, a sound of pure martyrdom. He's running out of ammo, I thought, if he has to resort to theatrics. Now's the time to quit this senseless war, this childish slinging of arrows.

"There was a Yaqui woman. She had a brother and a husband. Both of them got caught stealing horses one day. The judge said the penalty for horse-stealing was death by hanging. But the judge spoke to the woman. He said, "To lose both a brother and a husband would be terrible. So, you choose. Who will hang and who will live?"

The woman thought only a second before she replied, "Let my brother live for I can never get another brother, but I can always get another husband."

My daughters would have a strong mother. I looked at my husband and said as calmly as I could, "Please, don't slam the door as you go out."

SCOTT KAYLA MORRISON

A Memory of My Sister

IT WAS A PLOT TO RUIN MY LIFE. I KNEW IT, I JUST KNEW IT. Here Mom was, humming as she ironed Ramona's dress. Humming, do you believe it? The worst day of my life and Mom is humming. Ramona kept telling me to go away and not bother her. The day I needed them they were too excited to be bothered with me. Traitors, both of them.

My sister, Ramona, was starting first grade the next day. Mom's first child was beginning to flap her fledgling wings. The empty nest was still 28 years away from Mother, but her journey was beginning. Ramona's education, which lasted beyond the typical 12 years, would start the next day. But at four and a half, I was too young to be philosophical. I was just hurt and angry at losing my best friend and playmate. And she was leaving me with Mom's blessing. Shocking!

Ramona was up early the next day, barely sitting still long enough to eat breakfast. She would meet our cousins a quarter of a mile away. Together they would all cross the creek near our cousins' house and walk the rest of the way to Goss School together. Just as Dad and Duggan and all their brothers and sisters had walked to Goss School when they were little.

Dad's brother lived on the old home place in a house built after the house Dad and Uncle Duggan and everybody were raised in, burned years ago. I never knew when or how the "old home place" burned. It never seemed important to me since this happened when Dad was young and way before I was born. The family just called it the "old home place." I sometimes, but not often, wondered how Aunt Sis, a non-Choctaw, felt about living in the "old home place," instead of "Sis and Duggan's place." She somehow lost her identity when Duggan decided to build a house for her on the old home place.

Aunt Sis and Mother, married Choctaw men and lived on Grandma's allotment with their husbands and the rest of Grandma's kids. I guess Mom lost her identity, too. It happens when you marry Choctaw men and bear Choctaw children on the mother-in-law's allotment. Lost a lot of control over our upbringing too. I remember spending as much time at Grandma's or her daughters' houses as at my own. They taught me a bunch of stuff which I still remember, better than I remember the stuff Mom taught me.

The houses were pretty close together too, which worked out great for me and Grandma as she got older. Didn't have to walk far. Maybe that is why everybody kinda bunched up on one side of Grandma's allotment.

Grandma's allotment was at the foot of an eastern Oklahoma mountain and skirted Jack Fork's Creek. I used to think that if the allotment was a checker board, with all of us weighing down one side, we would tip the sucker over if the mountain was not there to catch us. But then, you see things differently when you're four, especially if you are an in-betwixt grandchild with no other grand-children close in age to play with. Which brings me back to my problem the day Ramona started school.

Mom's humming was intermittent with a slight clucking noise. Here, your belt isn't straight. Do you have on clean underwear? Gee, Ma, she's only going to school, not to meet the Queen or something.

"Come straight home after school." Naw, Ma, she'll run away with gypsies, or take to robbing banks. Of course, she'll come straight home. She knows I'll be stuck here all day with nobody to play with but you and Tom. And you are too busy and all Tom does is eat, sleep, and wet his diaper.

Ramona finally managed to get enough breakfast down to satisfy Mother that she wouldn't die of malnutri-tion before lunch. She kept re-arranging her pencils and paper in her satchel, like they were the most important items in the world, and world safety depended on their correct order in the bright, red satchel.

"Hurry up or you'll miss the other kids. I don't want you to walk alone."

Well, Mom, I'll set your mind at ease and walk with her to Aunt Sis's. No, don't thank me. Shucks, I've got nothing better to do.

"No, you need to stay here. We'll be able to see her all the way to your aunt's. Now, Ramona, you got every-thing? Remember to...no, you'll be fine without me tell-ing you how to behave. Give me a hug, baby."

Baby? Ramona? Boy, is Mom ever dumb! Ramona

isn't any baby, I have to look up at her, she's so tall. She can climb a tree to the very top. Then hang on while she hammers a board to make a tree house. She can pick out the best spot for a playhouse. And then find a better spot tomorrow.

And smart. Ramona knows to take off our shoes and socks at the bank of the pond so Mom won't know we've been playing in it because we're not supposed to. She knows a short-cut between our house and our cousins', so we can play longer and still get home when Mom said.

She can tie a rope to make a swing. Then push me so high. Mom's confused in her old age. Ramona's no baby. She's so strong, and brave, and smart; anything but a baby. And she was going to school. I will miss my best friend.

That first day was the longest of my life, and probably Mother's, too. Now that I have children of my own, I realize I probably drove her crazy asking when Ramona would come home.

Mom tried to give me some grasp of the alien concept of time that day. Ramona would be home when the big hand is on 6 and little hand is on 3. As she was washing dishes, I set about changing the hands to the magical positions to make Ramona appear.

"It don't work, Mom. The big hand is on 6 and the little hand is on 3. And she ain't here."

"You have to let the hands change by themselves. If you change them, it won't work."

"Why?"

"Well, trust me on this, it just won't work. She will be home when the Mickey Mouse Club comes on this afternoon."

"But that's zillions and gadzillions of years away. What will I do in the meantime?"

"You can ..." Mother began listing activities to keep me from underfoot. I'm sure she missed Ramona as much as I did. When Ramona was here, Mom always wondered where we were, instead of having me glued to her side like that day.

Afternoon finally came. Mom put up the ironing board and plugged in her iron. I was probably chattering about something because the next thing I remember was sitting under the ironing board, listening to Mom sing. There was something strange about this and it took me awhile to figure it out. Mom had set up the ironing board so we could both see out the door facing Aunt Sis's. I could sit cross-legged under the board, listen to Mom and watch for Ramona, all at the same time. Mom stopped singing, probably because I kept interrupting to ask another question. She started spelling my name, letter by letter, and I'd repeat it, over and over. Before I knew what she was doing I was spelling my name.

"Look out the door."

Ramona! I was off like a shot. We met at the edge of the yard. She was like a conquering hero returning with wondrous war stories of the first day of school. She should have a deserving welcome home. She didn't disappoint me either; she had stories. As I listened, it oc-

219

curred to me she missed me, Mom, and Tom as much as we missed her. At least she acted happy to be home with me, her biggest fan.

I followed her to school two years later. I somehow survived without my playmate for that length of time. But the real accomplishment is that Mother survived me being home with only a baby to play with for two years. Gritty woman, my mother.

Now at age 40, Ramona's first day at school is one of the few pleasant memories I have of my sister since I was four and a half. Our relationship is another victim to the white man's "gift" — alcoholism. No, you won't find it listed as any statistic on Native Americans' struggle with alcoholism.

Our relationship died without much fanfare years ago. You see, she followed Dad's path to alcohol abuse and I followed my own path to Al-Anon and abstinence. We are both Adult Children of an Alcoholic. We grew up in the same house and were only 22 months apart. Yet how we choose to deal with our crippling disease is so far apart, we can no longer communicate. And the truly sad part is I ceased crying about it years ago.

Carol McFadden

For Crystal

I FIRST NOTICED CRYSTAL WHEN ROSE POINTED HER OUT TO me. She was with a white man and her arm was in a sling. Her hair was straight, black, and hung down to her shoulders. Her pants were tight and her blouse was too small. Rose said she hated her. "Slut," that's what she called her. Crystal was in the corner of the club as if she wished no attention drawn to herself. Their table was almost behind the stage and speakers that the loud band was utilizing. There were beer glasses strewn all over the table in varying degrees of use.

Then I heard a loud crash. She had fallen on top of her man, their lips locked together, oblivious to the attention they had just drawn to themselves. There were beer glasses flying and the table was on its side. Everyone at my table laughed and pointed at her and the spectacle she was making of herself. We were thinking she had no pride, as we ourselves do. We ordered more paralysers, ciders, and long island ice teas, looked the other way and patted ourselves on the back for not being like her.

I last noticed her at the end of the night when all the lights came on. There she was crouched down on the floor, pants around her ankles, eyes cast shamefully down on her hands, which held her feet. Not moving, not saying a word, just sitting there. What? I could not comprehend how this had happened! Where was her man?

The people at my table and soon others around us were laughing so hard we couldn't even talk; we would merely point and laugh harder. Then, one by one, the bouncers came by, they would look, shake their heads and leave. Soon there was a huddle of bouncers wondering what to do with her. After much thought and apparently no answers they approached our table asking for assistance in getting her up and out the door. In response they were given more laughter. Finally they just ignored her and pretended she didn't exist.

What was she doing there? Some said she was peeing, others said she was fucking. Either way her man left her there, never to return. Her arm in a sling, of course, made it impossible for her to stand up and pull her pants up without exposing herself to all who watched and waited. So there she sat, eyes downcast, quiet, cornered with no way out. "Shut up," I screamed suddenly just as ashamed of myself as she was. "What's the matter with you? She's an Indian just like we are!" Help her! My mind screamed at me accusingly. I could not help her by myself. I needed someone to hold a coat up to shield her, which would then leave me to help her pull her pants up. Then, frantic, I ran from native woman friend to native woman friend pleading for help. I was greeted with laughter and disdain.

Time was running out, and I feared for her safety, as I saw the bouncers closing in. I ran back to tell her that I would try to find help, but on my return she was half standing, half sitting using her one free hand to first yank up one side of her pants, then the other, back and forth, inch by inch. I quickly grabbed my coat to shield her and she finished pulling her pants up. She did not acknowledge that I was even there, and I did not wish to humiliate her further so I turned around and sank into my chair.

I left the bar feeling ashamed that I had not helped her when I first noticed her. Ashamed that I, too, had laughed and pointed.

Articles & Non-Fiction

SUSAN BEAVER

Gays and Lesbians of the First Nations

This article is dedicated to all those who have gone before us to the spirit world and to all our Grandmothers, without whom we would not be here physically or culturally.

GENERATIONS BEFORE THE EUROPEANS INVADED TURtle Island our Grandmothers and Grandfathers, our ancestors, lived, breathed, held ceremonies, and governed themselves according to the complex demands and gifts of the land, our Mother. It was, and continues to be, a life rooted in respect, spirituality and a little bit of humour.

Before the Europeans invaded Turtle Island there lived the Berdache, the cross-dressers and the two-spirited people, in a respected and vital place in the societies of the ancestors. "Two-spirited" is a positive, traditional term that we prefer to call ourselves. What heterosexual people achieve spiritually in marriage, the union of two beings, we achieve by simply being ourselves. Creator made all beings spiritual beings but Creator gifted some of us to carry two spirits — male and female. Before the invaders we were the healers or medicine people, the visionaries and the blessed. For 500 years the colonizers have been trying to stamp out the First Nations people. And we have survived. Our cultures, languages, land, governments, and children have all been the subject of

227

attack. One of the first things the Europeans used to justify our inherent inferiority to their ways, and subsequently their most vicious attack, was the two-spirited people. And we have survived.

Today we come together after a long, hard road on which we still travel. Our strength lies in our collective heritage as First Nations people. Like First Nations people everywhere, we are still feeling the effects of colonization. Some of us can't speak our language, some were raised as Roman Catholics, and others stolen outright from their people. We come together with our varying degrees of knowledge and hope both to learn as well as to share. We learn what it is that makes us unique as Nations and as individuals.

We come together as social creatures (witness our tea and bannock get togethers) to forge stronger links. We learn of similarities as First Nations people and our differences as men and women. We come together as educators, for example Gay and Lesbians of the First Nation's "Aboriginal Women and AIDS" community forum. We have gone out into our own communities and talked about what it is to be two-spirited, to be HIV positive, to risk rejection by our family and community. We speak of acceptance and respect.

Like many communities, we have been affected by AIDS. Our response has been that only Native people can talk to Native people about our sexuality, our lives, and our futures with any understanding. This is very much in line with principles of self-determination for

Aboriginal people. Our response has taken us to high school classrooms, reserves, to our own leaders and to nurses. We ask you, the reader, to take time at this point to honour and remember the ones already taken by AIDS.

As First Nations people and as two-spirited people, we struggle to maintain our circle in a society that does not value the First People of this land. It is our intention as an organization to strengthen our cultures and reclaim our place in society. It is also our intention to laugh at ourselves and at life, the entire journey. Ny-weh/Meegwetch.

JANICE GOULD

A Maidu in the City of Gold: Some Thoughts on Censorship and American Indian Poetry

WHEN I STAND IN THE CITY OF GOLD, BUILT ON SAND, refuse, and the bones of my ancestors, something happens to me. As if looking at an old photograph, I see the amazing sand dunes that arose here out of the pressure of water, wind, and earth. The dunes are ridged like a whale's ribs, and yellow flowers break through the grainy surface of the earth on watery and tenuous roots. Fog gathers on the ocean, and in it are the voices of the dead. Tattered ghosts break off from the fogbank and collect along the edge of the bay to sing and dance and mourn, to pray for all that is passing away and for all that has to struggle into existence, into forms both beautiful and grotesque. I think of what is lost, of what has left this world, never to return: ancient beauty kept powerful and alive in the rounds of human and non-human generations, in rituals of renewal participated in by all who once inhabited this world.

When I stand in the City of Gold, I see the earth as it was, unravaged, miraculously healed and unscarred, not unchanging, not untended, but wholly itself, and belonging to itself. The hillsides are covered with oak and elderberry, with poppies and brodeaia, with tanbark oak, cedar, and madrone. The flocks of birds are yet here, pulled by the mysterious forces of survival. In hundreds of thousands, they inhabit the salt marshes and tule flats where freshwater creeks open in the bay, streams so clear and cold the salmon slip up them into icy spawning grounds fished by the grizzly bear, that fierce ancestor whose humpbacked shape gave definition to these hills. Deer come down from the thickets, and elk, and antelope with flicking tails. The herds cover the inland river valleys, stray along the northern reaches of the bay, nibbling the sweet grasses and owl's clover. And among this diversity of life are the Miwok, the Maidu, the Yokuts, the Ohlone, the Pomo, the Kato, Wailaki, Hupa, Yurok, Yana, Atsugewi, the People, many of us, generations living here on Turtle's back, surrounded by the great sea. Boats made of tule float on the tamal where the men fish and take oysters, and wherever large granite slabs jut from the face of the hills, women break down acorns to grind into meal. The Earth smells of mud, of sun, of clouds and rain, of smoke and stones and grasses. It smells of memory, and it gives back songs, language, existence.

This is the centre of the world, created in as many ways out of darkness and silence as there are a People to dream its origin. Cree poet Joy Harjo writes of another landscape near Shiprock:

> My house is the red earth; it could be the centre of the world. I've heard New York, Paris, or Tokyo called the centre of the world, but I say it is magnificently humble. You could drive by and miss it. Radio waves can obscure it. Words cannot construct it, for there are

some sounds left to sacred wordless form.[1]

The centre is not the City of Gold; it is a place "magnificently humble." And in time immemorial, that measure of existence that has no definite beginning, middle, or end, each People's story made this claim. Through language, and something beyond language, we were located in an incredibly permeable reality that shifts between the spirit world and this corporeal world of bones, flesh, food, breath, and thought. Through language, and something beyond it, this world was given being, dreamed and spoken into existence to answer who we are, why we are here, how we should live, and where we go when we leave. Here is an order of reality that seeks connection and community as a primary goal of living and insists on respect as a requisite of good behaviour.

But it is not just that, and it is not that easy, as Laguna writer Leslie Marmon Silko reminds us in her novel *Ceremony*.[2] It is a story of problematical return, renewal, and regeneration. Tayo is a young veteran who survives a death march in the Philippines during World War II. He comes back to his home at Laguna Pueblo at the close of the war sick and jaded, which is to say stained and drained by the outside world. Tayo returns to a land that has suffered years of drought. And what he needs to learn is his part in both the creative and destructive forces that are always at play in this world. When old Ku'oosh, the Laguna medicine man tells Tayo that the world is "fragile," Tayo is not prepared yet to handle what that means. Silko writes:

> The word he [Ku'oosh] chose to express "fragile" was
> filled with the intricacies of a continuing process, and
> with a strength inherent in spider webs woven across
> paths through sand hills where early in the morning
> the sun becomes entangled in each filament of web. It
> took a long time to explain the fragility and intricacy
> because no word exists alone, and the reason for
> choosing each word had to be explained with a story
> about why it must be said this certain way. That was
> the responsibility that went with being human, old
> Ku'oosh said, the story behind each word must be told
> so there could be no mistake in the meaning of what
> had been said; and this demanded great patience and
> love. (Silko, 35-36)

But just as in time immemorial the way to correct a
violation was no easy task, Tayo must go through his
own continuing process to learn, grow, and finally heal.
His regeneration and healing parallels and becomes a
contemporary version of those Laguna stories told from
time immemorial about violation and loss, about the
consequences of disrespect, disregard, and forgetfulness
of our Mother earth. This is indeed a fragile world, intimately interconnected. And Silko's novel must be read,
not only as an anti-war novel from the seventies, but also
as a brilliant ecological critique. It is, as well, a novel
about the colonial experience, about a colonized people

whose disenchantment and confusion allow them to participate and collude, unwittingly perhaps, in the greatest scientific contribution to potential world annihilation. For the mining of uranium on Laguna land provided the raw material used to construct the bombs that fell on Hiroshima and Nagasaki — a staggering thought.

But if you think Silko's novel is unique in its treatment of the question of colonization, think again. That is a great part of what our literature, American Indian literature, is about: dealing with the consequences of conquest, exploitation, and oppression. And as I stand here in the City of Gold, in which temples have been constructed as large as cathedrals in praise of the white man's enterprise, wealth and ingenuity, I wonder, how did anyone learn to want this? How did anyone learn to love this? Where has the spirit world gone, that rich world we enter in our dreams, from which we acquire knowledge and truth? And it occurs to me that we are the voices of the dead, we American Indian writers. I want you to hear some of the voices, here where we sit in the City of Gold. These are prayers disguised as poems, clothed in the oppressor's language, made respectable on the white pages of books. I will give you a history lesson to take with you when you step out on the street that paves the sandy hills and refuse and bones of my ancestors.

Reading the white man's history is an odd experience for an Indian. Many white historians whose focus is the history of the western United States tend to identify with the Spanish conquistadors, or at least tell a story that

adopts the explorers' perspectives or motivations. It is not
surprising, given that conquest and exploration were the
driving forces of American expansion, and still are. But
when we Indians read that we conquered ones were
people of "lowly stature,"[3] that as people we would be
subject to conversion, civilization, and exploitation we
represented both the means and the ends of conquest,[4] the
text and pretext for colonization, it becomes clear to us
that our experience of conquest has been necessarily
silenced and unacknowledged. That is what a poet like
Jimmie Durham from the Wolf Clan Cherokee tries to
rectify in a poem titled "Columbus Day."[5] In it, Durham
names the conquistadors as "filthy murderers," and links
them to our own illustrious military and backwoodsmen
in a momentary collapse of time when the relocation
policies of Eisenhower can be seen as equivalent to the
axing of Indians by good old Daniel Boone. Durham
names the People, the ones who lost their lives under
"Mr. Pizzaro's book." They were "Chaske," "Many
Deeds," and "Greenrock Woman," Durham tells us; the
woman "who walked right up/ And spat in Columbus's
face." I want to cheer that woman. In Durham's history,
she watched "Laughing Otter the Taino" being taken as a
slave, never to return. "Let us declare a holiday," writes
Durham,

> For ourselves, and make a parade that begins
> With Columbus' victims and continues
> Even to our grandchildren who will be named

In their honour.
Because isn't it true that even the summer
And every creek has accepted the responsibility
Of singing those names? And nothing can stop
The wind from howling those names around
The corner of the school.(130)

But are you listening? Or has the outrageous hum in the City of Gold stopped your ears? That is what I want to know. Because I worry when I hear about the caribou herds in Alaska, how vulnerable they are occupying a landbase that is seen and measured primarily in terms of its potential for creating wealth for already rich human beings. And probably most of us were sickened when we heard about the freighter Exxon Valdez spurting oil like a busted artery into Prince William Sound. But can we stick it to the oil industry for this and every other spill? Can we hold any of them accountable? The oil fires continue to burn in Saudi Arabia; the Persian Gulf has been reduced to a sewer. It is all connected in this fragile world: our crappy way of thinking gives us a crappy world to live in.

The warnings are everywhere. Listen to what Chickasaw poet Linda Hogan says in her poem, "Workdays":

I go to work
though there are those who were missing today
from their homes.

I ride the bus
and do not think of children without food
or how my sisters are chained to prison beds.
I go to the university
and out for lunch
and listen to the higher-ups
tell me all they have read
about Indians
and how to analyze this poem.
They know us
better than we know ourselves. (Niatum, 203)

Doesn't anyone get tired of trying to figure out what we're really saying? Isn't anyone besides me tired of analyzing poems, those artifacts closed to sacred texts that speak of the sanctity of life, or the pure meaning of existence, or of anguish and righteous anger and pain? What Hogan says in these spare couplets about living in a Minneapolis apartment, I take at face value:

I think of Indian people here before me
and how last spring white merchants hung an elder
on a meathook and beat him;
he was one of the People. (Niatum, 205)

What is to analyze? We live in a racist and violent society in which the war on Indians and other minority peoples continues unabated. That is what our poetry is about. That is what our novels are about. They are cries against that kind of brutality and oppression and annihilation of personhood and identity.

Indian writers do not mince words. If we are being published now in greater numbers than ever before, still we face the actual potential of being silenced, especially if we are gay or lesbian writers. Menominee writer Chrystos, who grew up in the City of Gold, was one of those blacklisted by Jesse Helms as being, in his opinion, a poor candidate to be awarded a fellowship from the National Endowment for the Arts. Her work is raw and to the point. It is about incest, rape, and mutilation: it is the modern day story of conquest, of that missionary zeal to annihilate the body and save the everlasting soul. The truth is that souls are intimately tied to the body, into the structure, fibre, and being of the body. On some level, I think all Indians must be survivors:

> Incest Keeps on Keepin On
> pushing my shoppin cart of rocks
> to that dragon of love leanin against a wall
> clear & dark
> I can't eat what's on sale my back hurts
> lost my shoes give any girl
> skin off my back hands mouth
> I'm your average pushy dyke stud lookin for legs to
> spread
>
> thinkin it'll get me a free meal soft bed home
> for a moment until a blonde comes along

Glass is cracked rain leaks in my tongue throbs
Aching beatup tin heart pushed aside
I'm buying time
Don't ask me to love you
I only know how to lay you / hate you / please you
underbelly I learned from twelve to twenty-one
lyin under him lyin
pushin his rocks off me / in me / down my throat /
up my ass

this hurt is dark deeply embedded
sell me a little solitude self-respect surprise
Humpin you is my way to forget
it's all I know how to do [6]

It's odd that Jesse Helms can't see the value of this poem. Or perhaps he does, only too well. But he would not be any happier reading Joy Harjo's poem, "For Anna Mae Pictou Aquash, Whose Spirit Is Present Here and in the Dappled Stars (for we remember the story and must tell it again so we may all live)."[7] This poem touches on the same kind of violence that Chrystos's poem elucidates, but it is also about censorship, about silencing. A footnote to the poem gives the history of the event: the body of an unidentified young woman was found on the Pine Ridge Reservation; the F.B.I. severed her hands from her body and sent them to Washington for fingerprinting. Later, when Anna Mae, a member of the American Indian

Movement, was found missing, the unnamed body was exhumed and a second autopsy was performed. It was then discovered that the young woman was Anna Mae Aquash, "killed by a bullet fired at close range to the back of her head. Her killer or killers have yet to be identified." Characteristic of Harjo, the poem emerges out of the dream, out of the space of prayer which is nothing less than seeing again how in the spirit world our ancestors continue to dance with a vision that will never be forgotten. Harjo says:

> Anna Mae,
>> everything and nothing changes.
> You are the shimmering young woman
>> who found her voice,
> when you were warned to be silent, or have your body cut away
> from you like an elegant weed.
>> You are the one whose spirit is present in the
>> dappled stars.
> (They prance and lope like coloured horses who stay with us
>> through the streets of these steely cities. And I
>> have seen
>> them nuzzling the frozen bodies of tattered drunks
> on the corner . . .)
>
> I heard about it in Oklahoma, or New Mexico,
>> how the wind howled and pulled everything

down
in a righteous anger.
(it was the women who told me) and we
understand wordlessly
the ripe meaning of your murder.
As I understand ten years later after the slow
changing
of the seasons
that we have just begun to touch
the dazzling whirlwind of our anger,
we have just begun to perceive the amazed world the
ghost dancers
entered
crazily, beautifully.

The Ghost Dance was a vision given in the 1800s to Wovoka, a Paiute ranchhand from the ravaged state of Nevada. In this vision, an apocalypse would wipe the white people from the face of the Americas, and the land, plants, and animals — everything that had been taken from the Indian — would return. All the relatives who had died at the hands of white men — from their diseases, their deceits, and their murders — would come back. The harmony of the earth would be restored, and Indians would be happy again.

The vision failed in the massacre of Lakota children, women, and men at Wounded Knee on December 29, 1890.[8] But after that happened, the Ghost Dance spread throughout nearly every tribe in the West, including many tribes in California. Perhaps something like the Ghost Dance was even performed here by the edge of the bay, somewhere near where the City of Gold has grown up on the sand hills, and refuse, and on the bones of my ancestors. Certainly, the Dream Dances of the Wintu people grew out of contact with the Pomo's Bole-Maru cult which descended from the Ghost Dance. In *The Way We Lived, California Indian Reminiscences, Stories and Songs,* Malcolm Margolin, the editor of the book, writes that the dream songs were given to dream by "dead friends and relatives . . . "[9] These songs "were often hauntingly beautiful." Perhaps the most poignant censorship of all for American Indians is to be divorced from the landbase that gave us all these songs, prayers, hopes and dreams. The long history of removals and relocations has not ceased. The Wintu song goes:

> Down west, down west we dance.
>
> We spirits dance.
>
> Down west, down west we dance.
>
> We spirits dance.
>
> Down west, down west we dance,
>
> We spirits weeping dance,
>
> We spirits dance.

ENDNOTES

1. Joy Harjo and Steven Strom, *Secrets from the Centre of the World* , (Tucson: Sun Tracks and The University of Arizona Press, 1989), 2.

2. Leslie Silko, *Ceremony* , (New York: Viking Penguin 1977), 43.

3. George P. Hammond, "The Search for the Fabulous in the Settlement of the Southwest," in David J. Weber, editor, *New Spain's Far Northern Frontier*, (Albuquerque: University of New Mexico Press, 1979), 31.

4. Herbert Eugene Bolton, "The Mission as a Frontier Institution in the Spanish-American Colonies," in David J. Weber, editor, New *Spain's Far Northern Frontier*, (Albuquerque: University of New Mexico Press), 51.

5. Jimmie Durham, "Columbus Day" in Duane Niatum, editor, *Harper's Anthology of 20th Century Native American Poetry* , (San Francisco: Harper and Row, 1988), 129.

6. Chrystos, *Dream On*, (Vancouver: Press Gang Publishers, 1991), 63.

7. Joy Harjo, *In Mad Love and War* , (Middletown: Wesleyan University Press, 1990), 7.

8. James Mooney, *The Ghost-Dance Religion*, (Chicago and London: The University of Chicago Press, 1965), 115.

9. Malcolm Margolin, *The Way We Lived, California Indian Reminiscences, Stories and Songs*, (Berkeley: Heyday Books, 1981), 176.

MARILOU AWIAKTA

Cherokee Eden
An Alternative to the Apple

MYTH IS POWERFUL MEDICINE. FOR CENTURIES, THE proverbial "Eden apple" has rolled through Western culture — the arts, politics, theology, society — and pointed its accusing, wounding stem at woman: "You are to blame for sin and destruction. You deserve to be punished." I refuse the apple. Instead, I reach for the strawberry — the powerful, healing medicine of Cherokee Eden. This myth has endured perhaps twenty-five hundred years, as long as the Cherokee themselves: Here I have adapted it from James Mooney's *Myths and Sacred Formulas of the Cherokee.*

The Origin of Strawberries

The first man and woman lived in harmony for a time. Then began to quarrel.

The cause is not told — the lovers themselves probably didn't know *exactly* — but the quarrel must have been long and tedious, for...

At last the woman left and started off to the Sun Land in the East where the Sun, being female, would likely comfort her.

The man followed, alone and grieving, but the woman kept steadily ahead and never looked back. The Provider (Creator), took pity on the man and asked him, "Are you still angry with the woman?"

He said, "No."

"Would you like to have her back again?"

He eagerly answered, "Yes."

The Provider doesn't ask the cause of the quarrel. Blame and punishment are not the concern. Healing is. In essence, the Provider asks the man, "Is your heart still hardened against the woman?" A crucial question, for a hard heart blocks reconciliation and abets mental/physical abuse. Only after the man affirmed his good intent does the Provider give help, using gentle persuasion.

The Provider caused many things to spring up in the woman's path:

A patch of ripe huckleberries. But the woman passed them by.

A clump of blackberries. The woman refused to notice.

Other fruits and then some trees covered with beautiful red service berries. The woman kept steadily on.

Last came a patch of large ripe strawberries, the first ever known. The woman stooped to gather a few to eat and as she picked them she chanced to turn her face to the west. At once the memory of her husband came back to her. She sat down, but the longer she waited the stronger became her desire for her husband. At last she gathered a bunch of the finest berries and started back along the path to give them to him. He met her kindly and they went home together.

Reconciliation. Healing. Acceptance of the human tendency to quarrel. A pattern for restoring harmony that involves mutual responsibility and restitution. This is Cherokee Eden, the powerful medicine of the strawberry.

The medicine will not work out of context, however. To experience the myth fully, one must understand its resonance — the ways of the people who gave it voice. The classic Cherokee culture was matrilineal. It was organized around the concept that the gender who bears life should not be separated from the power to sustain it. There were seven mother clans. In marriage, the man took the name of the woman's clan, as did their children. The woman owned the house. In divorce, which could be initiated by either party, the man returned to his mother's clan.

Women also planted, harvested and cooked — not as "squaw work," but as a crucial service to the people, for women were thought to have a special affinity for our Mother Earth. They also sat on the council and made their views known through the Beloved Woman, who shared the place of honour with the war and peace chiefs, both male. In matters concerning hostages, her word was absolute and she was believed to bring messages from the Provider to the people. It is through that, like her distant Iroquois relatives, who were also matrilineal, Cherokee women trained prospective chiefs. It is certain they helped shape government, which was collaborative rather than adversarial. Only in time of national emergency did the chiefs make arbitrary decisions. Otherwise, they guided by persuasion, and decisions were made by consensus. When a Cherokee chief squared off with a chief from another tribe, a delegation of women often functioned as intercessors. At its zenith in the mid-eighteenth century, the Cherokee nation extended into eight southeastern states. Although towns were widely separated and independently governed, they never warred with each other, for each town contained families from the seven clans. It was sternly forbidden to make war on relatives.

In the mythology of such a society, women naturally had an important place. Selu, the Corn Mother, for example, brought the first corn to the people, a cardinal physical and spiritual gift. Kanati, the Lucky Hunter, her husband, was the mythic father of mankind and brought hunting and woodlore to the people. Other myths explored the strengths and weaknesses of both genders, giving women as well as men prototypes for wholeness. If ideas of the Eden apple variety ever rolled in this culture, it is safe to assume the woman quickly made cider of them.

In 1817, this classic way of life officially ended. For

two hundred years the Cherokee had tried to work out a harmonious coexistence with European settlers, adopting many of their ways. Periods of peace alternated with broken treaties and bloody battles. In a final effort at reconciliation, the Cherokee changed to the patrilineal, republican form of government. The sound of the rolling Eden apple drove matrilineal ways underground. Twenty years later, the Removal began and decimated the nation. Many people in the dominant culture predicted, "In a hundred years, there will be no more Cherokee."

But roots held fast: the Cherokee now number about sixty-five thousand. Both Wilma Mankiller, chief of the Cherokee Nation of Oklahoma, and Principal Chief Ross Swimmer believe in collaborative government and in leadership through persuasion rather than coercion. Matrilineal ways are greening again. They have strength and endurance, like myth. Both have been kept alive by two concepts the Cherokee share with other Native Americans. One is the view of time as a continuum, a fusion of past, present, future. Related to this concept is the oral tradition. By *speaking* their ways and myths, the people keep them immediate and relevant. The *sound* of the words themselves makes them live in the present.

For that reason I suggest you do something outside the western tradition of the essay, which usually is read silently. So that you can *feel* the powerful medicine of the strawberry myth, ask a friend to read it to you — just the italicized part, not my asides. Quiet your mind. Listen. Note where the resonance of the words causes your

thoughts to vibrate. (I'll do the same, then share my
thoughts with you. In the meantime, share yours with
your friend. When we come together again, the medicine
will be alive and at work.)

...I feel good — so good that I toss the apple over my
shoulder. In Cherokee Eden there is respect for the
female, her intelligence and her rights of choice — and for
the male too. Neither gender is put down or cast in an
adversarial role. Competition is removed.

What a resonant fruit, the strawberry! It touches
many other places in my mind:

...*A quarrel with my companion*: Neither of us knows
the cause, exactly. After thirty years together, it could be
almost anything. I've kept "steadily ahead" for three
days. I ought to sit down, gather a few berries...

...*Notes for a talk on race relations for the National Conference of Christians and Jews*: I think I'll tear up my notes, just
read the myth (without my asides) and let it resonate.
Whatever our races or religions, we all have in common
similar teachings about forgiveness, reconciliation, restitution. A Cherokee myth might provide a neutral stimu-
lus for consensus.

...*Rape case in this morning's paper*: "She was asking for
it," the defendant says. The Eden apple — still rolling,
still powerful. Depressing, how little cider we've been
able to make of it.

...*A quote I heard at a lecture entitled "Urban Problems: A
Holistic View"*: The speaker, an expert from MIT, gave a

fine presentation. He then opened discussion by saying, "Adversarial modes of thought are breaking down. But when we look around for collaborative models, we can't find any."

I suggested we stop looking only at patriarchal European-American traditions and try Native American ones, adding, "The founding fathers based much of the U.S. government on the Iroquois pattern."

"But," countered the speaker, "we're having problems with it."

"That's understandable," I said, "because the Founding Fathers left out a basic component the Iroquois always included — women."

The words from the myth that touch me most deeply are, "alone and grieving." In the communal Cherokee culture, the worst curse one person could call down on another was not death, but loneliness. Perhaps it is the worst curse in any culture. "Alone and grieving..." As I travel about the country, how often I hear that feeling expressed. It is part of the modern, fragmented life. Surely we should draw from available sources to heal this condition.

Like the earth and air, powerful medicines — the fruits of thought — cannot be owned by anyone. They are for sharing. Even the pain-dealing apple plays its part in the whole, which may be to spur us on in the evolution of the human spirit. Each of us carries in the basket of our mind the myths and symbols of many cultures. It would be unreasonable and unwise to suggest we shake them all out to make room for others. What we can do is lay alternatives among them. I offer the Cherokee strawberry, the healing myth of a people who, like our Mother Earth, have refused to die.

In *Walk in Your Soul*, Cherokee scholars Jack and Anna Kilpatrick correct Mooney's translation of the Cherokee word *une:hlanv:hi,* which aboriginal Cherokee most commonly used to designate the Supreme Being: The Provider. Mooney translated this word as "the Great Apportioner," equating the Supreme Force to the sun. This is a common error in Western thought — and just among ethnologists. What impressed me the most is that the Kilpatricks made the correction in a good spirit, with respect for the sincerity of Mooney's heart and for the overall excellence of his work. The ability to deepen understanding without disparaging is admirable — and rare in American society today. In my mind I marked this footnote, "food for thought."

Janet McCloud

Historical Uses And Contemporary Abuses of Alcohol and Drugs by Indigenous Americans

W HEN AMERICA'S FIRST BOAT PEOPLE, COLUMBUS and the others, came to the eastern shores of this continent, the European nobility claimed the land under the so-called "right of discovery," a totally now concept in Europe Before that time all lands were acquired by conquest. Colonists, having to fight the superior, powerful Indian Nations, later decided it might be a better policy to barter for land use.

But, nonetheless they began to learn many Indian customs, including ways of preparing the different Native foods. Now they call it Colonial cooking instead of Indian cooking.

The English leaders told their colonial leaders to keep their people away from the Natives as they had a peculiar mental view of being a free and sovereign people.

Eventually the colonists learned the concept of freedom and struck a blow against English rule: the American Revolution. Strangely enough Benjamin Franklin and Thomas Jefferson learned to speak every language of the Six Nations Iroquois. It was the Iroquois system of laws after which the U.S. Constitution was modeled. This truth is finally coming out after being suppressed for two hundred years.

The independent colonies made treaties with the Indian nations prior to the revolution. One is called the "Two Road Wampum Treaty" which states quite simply that there would be a bond of peace and friendship, that each would follow their own road, and that neither would try to govern, legislate, or tax the other. The U.S. also stated that they would never take the Indians' land without their consent and just compensation. The U.S. made over 400 treaties and thousands of agreements with the Indian Nations and tribes within the boundaries of the present United States. Few were honoured. They are still the law of the land because they are the original land titles, from which all land titles today are derived. If the treaties are no good then the titles are not secure. The U.S. broke treaty after treaty as land grabbers pushed ever westward, in their greed and hunger for Indian land and resources. The Indians were always blamed for the violence and bloodshed that ensued. Rarely do the history books proclaim Indians as "patriots" who fought valiantly to protect their people and land from the invasion force that seemed unending.

Indians were vilified as inhuman savages fighting against the pioneers in sneak attacks. "The only good Indian is a dead Indian!" was the war cry heard all over this land.

It might have ended differently if the Gatling gun had not been invented, or if the buffalo had not been deliberately killed off to force the mighty Sioux Nations into captivity and dependency. Even with the Gatling

gun, killing Indians was an expensive venture for the U.S.
It was costing the U.S. one million dollars per Indian
killed, so new ways to eliminate Indians were created.

Ethnocide and Genocide

Ethnocide is the deliberate destruction of an ethnic
culture by denying, prohibiting, or destroying through
coercion, miseducation, and other methods the language,
religion, traditions, customs, etc. of those people. Genocide is "the deliberate and systematic extermination of a
national or racial group" (Random House Dictionary,
1968). Genocide and ethnocide overlapped one another in
the mid-1800's. Missionaries set up boarding schools with
the approval of the U.S. government. Indian children
were forced to attend but most of them ran away, so a
new plan was set up to transport the Indian children
thousands of miles away from their homelands.

The Indian students' hair was cut off because long
hair was seen as a mark of Indian religious beliefs. They
were then dressed in foreign clothes, and made to march
in military fashion to school rooms, dining halls, etc.
Christian ministers taught the Indian children that everything in their traditional ways, customs, and religious
teachings was *evil* and that their ancestors were burning
in hell, which was graphically portrayed. Even their
foods had to be English-style, boiled and devitalized.
Many thousands of Indian children died in these concen-
tration camps far from home. A few brave ones ran and

found their way back home where they told stories of unbelievable brutality, including physical and sexual abuse.

The damage was done. Indian children who went through these boarding school systems did not fit into their traditional lifestyles when they returned home, and they did not fit into the White man's society which still excluded Indians. Signs in most public places read "No dogs or Indians allowed." Some states had laws that read, "Any Indian caught off the reservation after 6 p.m. could be shot!"

Social Norms for Alcohol Use

The social norm for consumption of alcohol for Whites was any time, any place, any amount. At first, the "Hang Around the Forts Indians" were allowed and even encouraged to consume liquor any time, any place, any amount, until they became intolerable nuisances, beggars, violent, etc. Public drunkenness was not allowed in Indian society. Liquor was not allowed except during religious rituals when the time and amount was regulated by the elders.

The first alcoholic Indians no longer knew and/or followed the traditional ways of rearing their children. They did not know about the "Law of Imitation," that says children copy the behaviour of their adults, and so a new pattern of life began, a destructive one.

A popular stereotype held by White Americans is

"the drunken Indian" who can't hold his liquor like a "Civilized Man." Other theories postulate that Indians drink because of low self-esteem, poverty, alienation, and/or a poor self-image. The extreme racist view says "injuns" drink because they are an inferior species. Early Pilgrims and so-called Puritans declared that Indians were not human beings, they were creatures spawned by the Devil. Indians, so it is said, have no "social norm" for the consumption of alcohol.

Indian peoples of the Americas did have alcohol, it was a natural fermented liquor, only about 4 percent alcohol, made from fruits, cacti, corn, and melons.

There were strict social norms for the proper times for use of alcohol. The alcohol and drugs were used to alter minds and moods during religious ceremonies and rituals which were mostly done in groups, although there were times when an individual had to do a ceremony alone. A ceremonial year was 260 days. The Central American Indigenous people had thirteen sacred ceremonies which lasted for twenty days each.

Public drunkenness brought severe penalties against the offender, especially if they were priest, noble, or student. The penalty was *death*. Commoners were given a second chance to change their erring ways. "No other culture in all recorded history has had such severe penalities for public drunkenness."[1] "Despite all these alcoholic beverages, intoxication remained rare among Indians. They used alcohol as they did other drugs, in a primarily religious context."

Other drugs commonly used in religious ceremonies are cocoa leaves, marijuana, mescaline, tobacco, and various barks and roots. Some tribes used wine made from cacti in manhood initiation ceremonies. The Smithsonian report written in 1920 on the "Native Use of Daturas" says that several tribes used Jamestown or Jimson weed, and their usage was determined by elder priests who knew the safe dosage.

Christian leaders demanded that the U.S. government stop the practices of Indian religions. There was no freedom of religion for the Indigenous peoples of the Americas for over one hundred years, until 1978, when the Indian Religious Freedom Act was passed by the U.S. federal government. Indians continued to practise their religious beliefs in secret. If they were caught they were severely punished, imprisoned, tortured and discredited among their own people.

Denying Indians the basic human right to worship the Creator in the ways they had followed from time immemorial did great damage to the social structure of Indian communities. Indians no longer had the safe norms and restrictions on the use of alcohol and drugs. They began to imitate White society, who drank whenever they wanted to with no limits.

Addicting Indians for Profit

Alcohol was also used as a means to steal land from the Indians or as a way to cheat them in trade. One of the first corporations in America was the American Fur Trading Company, owned by John Jacob Astor. Astor made his fortune in the fur trade. Rot gut liquor, diluted and adulterated with unspeakable pollutants, was provided to Indians for free at first, until they were addicted. Once addicted to alcohol, the Indians had to bring in furs for liquor. After Astor made his ill-gotten fortune he went to England and bought himself a title.

Indian leaders forbade any of the traders to bring liquor into their territories, but they were powerless to stop them from doing so.

There were certain areas where all tribes gathered at certain times of the year to trade. These sites were sacred ground, where no hostilities were allowed and hospitality was extended to all. It was to these sites that traders first came. Indian leaders were incensed at the traders for addicting their people. Indians who became alcoholics were exiled from their homelands and became known as "Hang Around the Fort Indians." One of the biggest complaints of Indian Leaders in these days was against liquor. They demanded that the U.S. stop the traders from coming into their terrorities with liquor. These prohibitions were incorporated into all the treaties made with the U.S.

Article 9 of the Medicine Creek Treaty of 1854 with the Nisqually, Puyallup, and other tribes states, "the above tribes and bands are desirous to exclude from their reservation the use of ardent spirits and to prevent their people from drinking the same..." (*Kapplers Laws and*

Treaties, Vol II, 663). To this day most Indian reservations still prohibit liquor sales.

Eventually the "Hang Around the Fort Indians" began to exhibit antisocial and sometimes violent behaviour resulting in White people's complaints about drunken Indians. Soon alcohol was forbidden to all Indians until 1953. Thus, Indians were the original prohibitionists, disdaining the use of alcohol outside of religious ceremonies long before the Temperance League or Carrie Nation.

Alcohol was used to cheat the Indians out of the ownership of their lands. In Tacoma, Washington unscrupulous land grabbers and many leaders in the White communities shouted and pushed the federal government into making the Puyallups citizens of the U.S. so that their lands would be put into fee simple title. This happened in the early 1900s. Many Puyallups were illiterate, unable to speak or write English.

Soon the Puyallup land was allotted out to individual land owners. It did not take long for the Puyallups to be cheated out of their land. Guests would visit the Indians, give them hard liquor and then when they were drunk, they had them put an "x" on a piece of paper. Then they kicked the Indian family off their land.

Truth About Our History

One must glean through hundreds of books to ferret out the truth about our history. We need hundreds of

Indian writers to write our history and to do studies about European culture and customs prior to their invasion of America. A people without history will always be victimized. They will believe the falsehoods, live the stereotypes. No child can feel proud of their ancestors when they are always depicted as bloodthirsty savages killing the pioneers.

Since the renaissance that took place in Indian Country in the 1960s there have been changes. Churches have given an apology for their historic crimes against Indians, a few court decisions have recognized treaty protected lands and resources, and Indian philosophies are being rediscovered all over the world. This will have a positive impact on the social pride and dignity of Indigenous Americans in their struggle to heal.

The original, free sovereign Indigenous people of the Americas bear the wounds and scars of five hundred years of oppression, genocide, ethnocide, discrimination, racism, bigotry, lies and falsehoods. It is not easy to forgive and forget, especially when blatant discrimination continues, i.e., the Treaty Beer issue, jails filled with proportionately more Indians than non-Indians because of alcohol-related crimes.

A tragic example of the state of Indigenous people in North America today is Robert Sundance, a Sioux Indian, now a recovering alcoholic. He spent 25 years on skid row. Three-quarters of his last ten alcoholic years were spent in city jails. Then, in 1970, he struggled to change the system that criminalized alcoholics. His court case,

Sundance versus Los Angeles Municipal Court, ended in victory. Alcoholism was determined to be a disease, not a crime. Police began placing alcoholics in detox, not jail.

Concerned Indian leaders and recovering alcoholics continue heroic work in an attempt to help their people deal with alcoholism and drug abuse. One day there will be a happy ending, but until then the struggle continues.

REFERENCES

BOOKS

Ackerman, Robert J. *Growing Up the Shadow*. Health Communications, 1986.

Barreiro, Jose. *Indian Roots of American Democracy*. Cornell University, 1988.

Driver, Harold E. *Indians of North America*, Second Edition. Chicago: University of Chicago Press, 1969.

Harlan, Judith. *American Indians Today*. Watts Publishing Co., 1987.

Waters, Frank. *Mexico Mystique: The Coming Sixth World of Consciousness*. Sage Books, The Shallow Press Inc., 1975.

Weatherford, Jack. *Indian Givers: How the Indians of the Americas Transformed the World*. New York: Fawcett/Columbine, 1988.

Wilson, Edmund. *Apologies to the Iroquois*. New York: Vantage Books/Random House, 1959.

PAPERS

The Geneva Conference, NGO Conference on Human Rights, United Nations, 1977.
Fourth Russell Tribunal, November, 1980.
Internal Federal Document, 1977.

INDIAN PUBLICATIONS

Akwesasne Notes, P.O. Box 196 Mohawk Nation, Rooseveltown, New York 13683-0196.

Day Break Newspaper, P.O. Box 98, Highland, MD 20777-0098.

Puyallup Tribal News, 2002 East 28th Street, Tacoma, WA 98404.

SOURCES NOT GENERALLY AVAILABLE

Smithsonian Report, Volume II, No. 18, American Ethnology, J.W. Powell.

Federal Handbook on Indian Law, Feliz Cohne.
Kapplers Laws and Treaties, Volume II, 1905 edition.

CHRYSTOS

Interview

TOO COLD TODAY TO SIT ON THIS BENCH & TALK. I'M riding the buses. Come back tomorrow.

Did you bring anything to drink? Well, I need a cigarette. Kills the pain. I don't want none of that granola crap. Chicken feed. Naw they don't let me in any of them cafes down here. I tell you they'd call the cops. Doesn't matter whether you have the money, they don't wanna LOOK at me. Don't you get it? Well then get me some Bailey's Irish Cream over at the state store. It's my favourite & I ain't had none in more than a year.

That's better. Oh it's just scabies. Long as we don't sleep together you won't get em. *Hey Hey Ha.* Want a sip? Doncha know how to have any fun? If talkin' to me is your fun, you had a worse life than me. I'm just like that bird over there on the bare branch, fluffin up my feathers to keep warm. That bird has a story, too. Probably seen as much death as I have. She doesn't have a job either. But she's cuter than me or something. Gets fed every day by this old Chinese lady with a bad limp. She's got crackers in packages from some restaurant. Her husband walks along ahead of her real stiff & sore. You have to watch them a long time to realize they're together. One time that lady came over to me when my eye was bleedin' from a fight me & Ted had & she said, "You should go to the doctor," and gave me a ten dollar bill. I don't know any ten dollar doctors myself, but I said, "Thank you, mam." That's when I had my last little bit of Bailey's. My stomach's so bad it's the only one I can keep down.

Yeah well that bird & that Chinese lady ARE the story of my life. OK, to please you. I was born in '43 over on the rez. My dad was killed in the war & my mom started drinking soon after that I guess, if she wasn't drinking before. I don't remember her too well because she died when I was seven. Those child protective services came & got me & I ain't been back to the rez since. There ain't no tradition there I remember but drink & fights & death & misery. Sure ain't nobody to scam any money off. I do pretty good down here. Or I did til they put those signs up about givin' money to panhandlers can't help us. Stores just want all the money for themselves. Don't help us at all & we were here long before their little 88 dollar teacups and pointy noses.

Well I got the TB so who knows what's gonna happen. Naw I don't want nothing to do with hospitals. Nothing to do all day but stare at the ceiling & have a bunch of bitches treating you like shit cause they're treated like shit when you're laying down half naked & can't defend yourself. Government says I'm not even supposed to be alive anymore. Yeah they say Indian women only live to 47. So I'm doin' real good. I say any living Indian is a hero, ought to get a medal & a plaque & a grant no matter how messed up they are. I'm due for a grant myself. So you got one? You go to college?

They always said I was too dumb but I wanted to go,

wanted to learn how to speak all the languages in the world so I could understand what's happening. They said it was a CRAZY idea. Oh yeah I bin locked up off & on. But I know how to play their game. So I always get out. Yeah, you say, I was really crazy when you came & took me off the streets but you helped me so much & I'm better now. I'm gonna get a job soon as I get out & straighten up my life. You got to get the right tone of humble pie in there. Suckers go for that BS everytime. They ain't helpin' nobody but themselves. I don't need any help. I'm doin' fine. How would all these rich people know how much better off they think they are than me if I wasn't here? I'm part of the balance of the universe. Course then you have to leave town for a few months til they don't remember what you look like.

Oh I got a knife here in my boot. I cut the last guy pretty bad who tried that stuff. Called the ambulance myself cause it looked like he might bleed to death. Nobody's bothered me since. Word gets 'round same as it does anywhere.

Hey Kid, stir up any good trouble? Listen, stay away from that old white guy over there in the brown coat. He's mean to his bones. Hit people with that cane of his for no reason at all. Oh it's lead — weighted at the end, could kill you if he gets your head. Broke somebody's leg with it after you left last week. Young kid who wanted to hang out with us & find out about real life, didn't know nothing. *Hey Hey Ha.* Just like you. *Hey Hey Ha.* Naw they took him off to some hospital in the U district. Get this —

he said he wouldn't prosecute the homeless masses, now ain't that some shit. That old man ain't really bad, he just can't stand people. Doesn't want anybody to talk to him, get near him. Nothing. I'm sure he has a REAL good reason. I could be like that myself. Don't you get it? This SURELY is my life story. You think you live outside of my story? You're a part of me, too. This story is as much about you as it's about me. You think you're separate from me but you're right here on this bench now. You'll never forget this day or me & you'll probably dream about me tonight. There is no one story. We're all together. Some of us are just more uppity than others. More cold & mean.

What do you want to hear about all that for? I had so many foster parents I can't remember their names. Some of the dads raped me & some of the boys too. I've been raped but I've never been in love. Just don't have it in me to lose my mind that way. No, I never did have a job. Lived with guys back when I was pretty. Oh I got sterilized at the state hospital when I was 17 so I didn't have any kids. Sure my life would be better if I'd had kids. Well they keep you honest. They're a woman's gift to creation. Ever look in a child's eyes? Clear down to their soul, breathing the spirit of love. Everybody beats them, rapes them, lies to them, tells them to shut up, uses them, & that's how we get so twisted up the way we are. You know, when those people from Europe showed up here lost we were scared to death of them because we couldn't imagine anybody savage enough to beat their kids. I myself am still scared of most white folks & stay as far away from em as I can. Guess that's why they think we all vanished. *Hey Hey HA.*

Get rid of all them & there might be a change. We're so hurt we want our children to heal us & they're too little to do it. So we hurt them because we can't stand how clear they are, how easy they laugh, how easy they cry, how much they love everything & everybody until you teach em different. World going to the dregs way people buy kids every kind of plastic toy geegaw but never talk to them. Plastic can't bring anybody happiness. Not even that new & improved natural hippie plastic. I didn't talk til I was three. Some said I was retarded. Mom wasn't around, she didn't talk, how was I supposed to learn? No I don't think about her now. She got run over by some white guy, by accident, they say, walking back from the store. Nothing happened to him.

Look it's so cold the birds are all gone. Well if you give me money I can go over to the Y & get a little room for the night. Yeah & then I can get a shower, be great. OK, have beautiful dreams tonight yourself.

Say these are nice mittens thanks. No I don't wanna come & stay with you. I like my independence. We're sure to get on each other's nerves. I don't mind talkin' to you once in a while but I don't like you enough to live with you. No it ain't pride. Why should I waste my time making you feel good 'cause you think you rescued me? I like this life. This is the edge of the blade. I see the bottom of the river. I know exactly where I am. No illusions.

Nothing anybody can take away from me. You really on this thing aren't you? They gonna give you some money for writing about me? A copy of this in a book? You're kidding. NO I don't want one. You think I don't remember what I say? Don't need a book to know who I am. Books are too damn heavy & no good against the wind. Newspaper is much better. Yeah, I can read you don't have to insult me. I read lots of things & then I decided I like my own mind much better. Like to watch her fly. Sometimes I become a cloud & drift round all day. Books are for lonely people. I ain't never been lonely in my life. Got the sky. Best friend a person could have. Funniest book I ever saw was in Elliot Bay's window. Big deal about how they're destroying the rain forest & they destroyed a forest here to print it up. You see? Books don't make any sense. I'll take a baloney sandwich instead. So when this gets in a book, will you feel better, will you have a good time then? Well you better hurry up & start having some good times girl cause you're Indian too & ain't got too many years left yourself. *Hey Hey HA.* Don't get it do you? When you're dead that's it. I tell you have a good time now 'cause you sure don't wanna be in your grave pissin' & moanin'. You wanna be WORE OUT when you hit that dirt.

Well we could go over & shoot some pool at the tavern. They got sandwiches. Got a polka band there on Saturday nights for your kinda girls you know. Well you're a dyke ain't you? Nothin' to be ashamed of. There's plenty of ways to have fun. Tried it myself. Yeah I stayed with her long as I could. She wanted to be too settled down, make a little home with pink curtains & all that. I got to feel trapped. Later she sent me money to my box number til she died. Cancer. Yeah breast cancer. Kills most of us women. Our hearts & breasts hurt so much from how we're treated, how they treat the earth, all the air & food & water are full of poisons cause they got greedy white men running the whole world, that cancer just gets in our pain where we nurture and that's that.

You can't play pool?! Well then you better let me teach you. Come on.

Well, I never seen anything funnier than you trying to make a pocket last week. This is good soup, you make it? Hey my mom used to make bone soup too. Forgot all about that. Yeah a thermos is handy. OK well I could sure use it. You aren't giving me all this stuff because you feel sorry for me are ya? Well your daddy is a good man & he's right, more you give, more you receive.

I said you can't understand your life better by under-standing mine. Because you can never understand my life. Nobody but me can even try. You got more than you can do to understand yourself. Take you your whole life if you awake & you still may not know much when you get ready to kiss that dirt. We're rivers of blood in the same body, birds heading north in spring, clouds mov-ing. That's all there is to know.

The only reason we were brought together is so you could notice that bird I showed you. You got to start seeing where you are, not read so many books. Only your eyes or your dog if your eyes don't work, can get you from here to there, wherever there is gonna be.

Listen, Manny's going down to LA tomorrow in a car he got. Yeah he plays the guitar over in the market for the tourists. Now all that Santa Claus BS is over, business is lousy until June. So I won't see you again til summer. I want you to do me a favour. Keep coming to this bench once in a while to make sure that old Chinese lady doesn't slip on the ice. I want you to practise while I'm gone so you can actually hit something INTO a pocket when I'm back. Yeah I'm coming back. This is where Maizie's buried. Yeah she's the woman I told you about. I guess I did love somebody after all. Maizie Truvillon.

Why the hell are you crying? You CAN'T miss me 'cause I'm in your heart & dreams. If I kick the bucket, I'll tell Manny to let you know. This number be good until June? Maizie got me a plot next to hers. Now what do you think is suddenly gonna happen to me that I can't take care of? You've been around for two months that's it. I've been living and living before you came along for 53 years. You better worry about yourself. You got a big problem if you don't learn to have some fun. NO you can't come to LA with me & Manny. I already told you, you get too close. Hurts me to have anybody close. Yeah I'll be careful. I promise not to step in any dog shit if it's gonna make you happy. *HEY HEY HA.*

Now why should I send you a postcard? You afraid I'm not real or you're not real? This is real. Once you're in somebody's dreams you can't miss them anymore. Yeah I dreamed about you last night. You were trying to play pool in a hospital gown & red mittens & I was watching your back so nobody could see your cute bare ass hangin' out. I woke up laughing. Best way to start this day & this trip.

Instead of missing me why don't you practise flirting til I get back so you'll be a little better at it? Maybe we'll have some trouble of our own hey? Naw Manny & I aren't like that. Maizie is the last one I went with. Men are no good at it for me. Come too fast for me to have any fun. Sure I miss it. But women always want some romance with their sex & I'm not about to buy some diamond ring. Now is that why you wanted me to come & stay with you? *HEY HEY HA.* You're getting red as these mittens. You gonna put this in the book too?! You're crazy.

You know if we get into some nice trouble I ain't letting you put that in a book! I won't be able to beat the women away. *Hey Hey HA.*

Tell you what when I get back from LA I'll take you dancing at the polka place & buy you some of that weird juice you drink. Sure. Manny's got a buddy down there who works in a place making clothes. We can get brand new outfits just for hauling out the scrap bins. I'd better bring you some dancing shoes 'cause you sure ain't wearing those sneakers on a Saturday night. I'll give you a little hint. I can't resist a woman with flowers in her hair.

Here's Manny. Hey Man I see you could finally quit snagging long enough to show up. This is that girl I was tellin' you about who's gonna put me in a book after I put her somewhere ELSE HEY! I guess you might be in it too. Yeah that's a real good idea! Tell everybody reading the book that Anita and Manny say, HEY how you doin'?

Contributors' Notes

Annharte: is working on her poetry manuscript *Blueberry Canoe*. She's just completed a chapbook, *Coyote Columbus Cafe*. Her other writing projects include *Some of My Best Friends Are*, a CBC Fringe Radio Drama contest winner, *Alter-native* script for the Winnipeg Fringe Festival and touch ups on *Albeit Aborginal*, a real bannock back burner effort to send up instant Indigenous shake 'n bake spirituality/cultural appropriation. She's a part-time student/storyteller and a practising performance artist.

Jeannette Armstrong: is an Okanagan Indian. She is a fluent speaker of the Okanagan language, and she has studied traditional teachings and practiced traditional ways for many years under the direction of Okanagan Elders. She is a writer, sculptor, artist, teacher, and an outspoken Aboriginal Rights activist. After studying Creative Writing and receiving a degree in Fine Arts through the University of Victoria, she focused her work toward developing First Nations Educational Institutions. She is founder and former Director of En'owkin Centre and is currently the Director of En'owkin International Writing School. Armstrong has written a number of books including *Slash*, a novel, *Breathtracks*, a collection of poetry, and several children's books as well as various film scripts produced for television. Her collaborations with other First Nations poets and musicians have also appeared on several tapes and CDs including "Till the Bars Break." She recently co-authored, with renowned architect Douglas Cardinal, *The Native Creative Process*.

Marilou Awiakta: Cherokee/Appalachian poet and author who grew up on a reservation — for atoms, not Indians — Oak Ridge, Tennessee. The U.S. Information Agency chose her books *Abiding Appalachia: Where Mountain and Atom Meet* and *Rising Fawn and the Fire Mystery* for its 1986 global tour, "Women in the Contemporary World". For excellence in a body of work and service to the people she received the 1989 Distinguished Tennessee Writer Award. Her new book is *Selu, Seeking the Corn-Mother's Wisdom*.

Awiakta will be profiled in the 1994 *Oxford Companion to Women's Writing in the United States*. She lives in Memphis, Tennessee.

Shirley Bear: born on the Negootgook (as we know it) Tobique Reserve (as you titled and know it). Early schooling by the Roman Catholic Church through to high school at a residential school. No art degrees but a wealth of shared learning and expert knowledge by many of the better creative artists in the Americas. Shirley Bear has been an artist all her life and a political activist for about fifteen years. She has written poetry since she was a teenager but just recently started publishing. Today she is a full-time visual artist and writer and continues to be active for justice issues whenever and wherever necessary.

Janet Beaver: is a member of the Alderville First Nation near Rice Lake, Ontario. After a successful career with the Ontario Ministry of the Environment, Jan decided to start a second career teaching. She now teaches grade five in North York. Jan's spiritual path is shared by many Anishnawbe people of the Seventh Fire, to rediscover those things that have been lost along the trail, to rediscover how to live in harmony with Mother Earth and all of Creation.

Kathryn Bell: is a member of the Southern Cheyenne Nation. She is a journalist/writer by profession and is co-founder of American Indian Media Services, Inc. which provides media services (video and print) to American Indian tribes, organizations and businesses. She has worked 20 years exclusively with Indian tribal governments and organizations. She was born, raised, and has always lived in Oklahoma.

Kimberly Blaeser: is Anishinabe and an enrolled member of the Minnesota Chipewa Tribe. She grew up on White Earth Reservation. She is currently Assistant Professor in the English and Comparative Literature Department of the University of Wisconsin-Milwaukee. She has published personal essays, poetry, short fiction, and scholarly articles in various journals and anthologies.

Her book *Gerald Vizenor: Writing in the Oral Tradition*, and a collection of poetry *Trailing You*, will be published soon.

Jan Bourdeau (Waboose): is an Ojibway woman who has enjoyed writing stories and poetry from an early age. She has lived both on and off reserve. Jan has worked closely with Chiefs and Band Councils for many years. Her poetry was published in the anthology, *The Sweet Grass Road*, June 1993. Her first children's picture book will be published in Spring, 1994. Jan's inspiration comes from watching the leaves dance on the trees and listening to the wind singing through them.

Beth Brant: is a Bay of Quinte Mohawk from Tyendinaga Mohawk Territory in Ontario. She is the editor of *A Gathering of Spirit*, the ground-breaking collection of writing and art by Native women. She is also the author of *Mohawk Trail*, prose and poetry and *Food and Spirits*, short fiction. Her work has appeared in numerous Native, feminist and lesbian anthologies and she has done readings, lectures, and taught throughout North America. She is currently working on a book of essays titled *Testimony From the Faithful* a collection of her speeches and talks. She does work for her communities through writing workshops, mentoring programs, and working with Native women in prison to help develop their creative voice. She is a lesbian mother and grandmother.

E. Kim Caldwell: is Tsalagi, Creek, Shawnee, Celtic and German. She currently lives and works in Depoe Bay, on the Central Oregon Coast. Her work has been included in *The Returning the Gift Anthology*, and in *Healing the Spirit; Grandaughters Speak on Grandmothers*. She is author/narrator of *When the Animals Danced* performed internationally by the Pacific Dance Ensemble, Newport, Oregon. Currently she is editing and writing for the Native feature section of *Perpetua, the Magazine* and freelances work to other publications. She is currently the editor/writer of the Native section of *Inkfish* magazine.

Jeanetta L. Calhoun: is of mixed Lenape (Delaware) and European ancestry. She has published poetry previously in *Pig Iron*, *Sail*, and is accepted for publication in *Re-Inventing the Enemy's Language*. She also writes essays. Jeanetta is married and the mother of Michael, age 3.

Chrystos (Menominee): was born off-reservation in San Francisco on November 7, 1946. She devotes her life to the concept of justice with writing and art as expensive hobbies. She is author of *Not Vanishing* and *Dream On*. Also, a new collection of lesbian erotica, *In Her I Am*.

Nancy Cooper: is an Anishnawbe Kwe from the Rama Reserve in Ontario. For the past two years she has worked in Toronto within the First Nations community. She is an adult educator and activist. She writes because she can't help it. "Meegwetch. All my relations."

Elizabeth Cuthand (Cree): grew up in Saskatchewan and Alberta. She has taught at the Saskatchewan Indian Federated College, University of Regina since 1986. Before teaching, she worked as a journalist for sixteen years. Her short stories and poems have been published in magazines and anthologies, and two volumes of her poetry appeared as separate monographs, *Horse Dance to Emerald Mountain* and *Voices in the Waterfall*. She is currently doing graduate work in Creative Writing at the University of Arizona in Tucson, where she is also writing her first novel.

Kateri Damm: is a woman of mixed Ojibway, Polish Canadian, Pottawatomi, and English blood, and is a card-carrying Band member of the Chippewas of Nawash at Cape Croker, Ontario. She was born in 1965 and was reborn as a C-31 Indian in the 1980s. She received her B.A. in English in 1987 from York University and will receive an M.A. from the University of Ottawa as soon as she passes a French test. She recently coordinated *Beyond Survival*, an international conference of Indigenous writers, performing and visual artists. She is currently trying to establish a small publishing company to promote Native writing. Earlier this year, she published her first collection of poetry, *my heart is a stray bullet*.

Charlotte De Clue: Osage writer from the Territory, has been writing for fifteen years and recently published *Ten Good Horses*. She has been active in the religious freedom movement in particular and the rights of Native prisoners in Oklahoma. She is 45 years old, and is married to a Comanche Indian named Jerry Pelley. They are grandparents to a new baby girl named Maria Charlotte.

Marilyn Dumont: is Metis. She writes from her experience of being Native, a woman, and lower-class. She has been writing for an audience for twelve years and publishing for eight years in literary journals such as: *Blue Buffalo, CVII, A Room of One's Own, Newest Review* and in two anthologies: *Writing the Circle* and *The Road Home*. She is a freelance writer and video and film producer.

Carolyn Dunn: Writer, poet and playwright, born in Los Angeles, California in 1965. She graduated from Humboldt State University with a B.A. and received her M.A. from UCLA in American Indian Studies. Her non-fiction has appeared in *Belles Lettres, News From Native California,* and the forthcoming *The Oxford Companion to Women's Literature in the United States.* Her poetry has appeared in several publications including *Jacaranda Review, Toyon,* and the forthcoming *Recreating the Enemy's Language.* She is also author of a book of poetry *We Are At War.* She teaches Native American literature and theatre in the Native American Studies program at HSU. She is finishing a new novel, entitled *Deer Woman.* Carrie is a member of the Chickamauga Nation of Arkansas and Missouri, and is proud of her Creek, Seminole, Cherokee, African American, and Cajun ancestry, can cook a mean pot of gumbo, and speaks French (and some Muscogee and some Cherokee) with a great Southern accent.

Anita Endrezze: is half Yaqui Indian and half European (Slovenian, German-Romanian, and Italian). Her most recent book is *At the Helm of Twilight*. Her fiction and poetry appears in many anthologies, such as *Harper's Anthology of 20th Century Native American Poetry* and *Talking Leaves*. Her work has been translated into seven languages in ten countries. She has two children and is married to a Danish citizen but they live in the U.S.A.

Heid Erdrich: is Metis and a member of the Turtle Mountain Band of Ojibwa. Born in 1963 she was raised in North Dakota. She attended Dartmouth College and Johns Hopkins University. Heid teaches college writing and Native American literature classes and is an advocate for multicultural youth in education. She is a founding member of Native Arts Circle Writers of Minneapolis/St. Paul, a group currently editing a collection of Native writers from the Upper Midwest and Southern mid-Canadian region.

Colleen Fielder: was born in Ingonish Beach, Nova Scotia, in July 1946. She graduated from St. Francis Xavier University in Antigonish with a B.A. in English. Colleen wrote poetry since third or fourth grade. Books and writing were always important to her. After marriage Colleen and her husband Bob lived on the West coast. Colleen had three children, her pride and joy — Kyla, Jordan, and Lee Anne. Colleen died in a car crash in July, 1991 near their home on the Sunshine Coast in British Columbia.

Connie Fife: is a Cree writer from Saskatchewan. She is the author of *Beneath the Naked Sun*, a collection of her poetry. She was the co-editor of *Fireweed A Native Women's Issue*. She currently lives in Toronto with her son Russell, and her cat Grey Cloud.

Janice Gould: was born in San Diego, California, but grew up in Berkeley. She worked at various jobs before enrolling at the

University of California, Berkeley, where she earned a B.A. in Linguistics and an M.A. in English. She is currently finishing work on a Ph.D. in English at the University of New Mexico. She is the recipient of a grant from the National Endowment for the Arts, and from the Astraea Foundation. Her work has appeared in numerous anthologies of both American Indian and Lesbian writing, including *An Intimate Wilderness* and *A Gathering of Spirit*.

Leona Hammerton: is 38 years old, with five children, one stepson and is on her third grandchild. She is working for a B.A. in education at the Universtiy of British Columbia, a Native Internship Program. She worked this summer on the land claims issue as a land researcher. She is interested in Archeology and Anthropology and working to preserve some of her Native heritage through talking with elders.

Joy Harjo: was born in Tulsa, Oklahoma in 1951 and is an enrolled member of the Creek Tribe. She graduated in 1968 from the Institute of American Indian Arts and from the University of New Mexico in 1976. In 1978 she received and M.F.A. in Creative Writing from the Iowa Writer's Workshop at the University of Iowa. She has published four books of poetry including *She Had Some Horses* and the award-winning *In Mad Love and War*. *Secrets from the Center of the World* is a collaboration with photographer/ astronomer Stephen Strom. She is currently Professor of English in the creative writing program at the University of New Mexico. Joy has received the Josephine Miles Award for Excellence in Literature from PEN Oakland and the William Carlos Williams Award. Her forthcoming book, an anthology of Native American women's writing, *Reinventing the Enemy's Language*, will be published in 1993.

Linda Hogan: is a Chickasaw poet and novelist. Her latest book is *The Book of Medicines*. She also authored *Mean Spirit*. and is currently working on a new novel entitled, *Solar Storms*.

Ruth Huntsinger: (Lakota-Rosebud) Retired Indian Studies instructor at Black Hills State University and Mankoto State University.

Edna H. King: is Nishnawbe from Chimnihsing, presently living in St. Catharines. Some of her work has appeared in *Do Whales Jump at Night, Fireweed* and *The Adventure on Thunder Island.* In the spring of 1992, Edna's short story "Adventure on Thunder Island" won the Vicky Metcalf Award for Children's Short Story Writing from the Canadian Author's Association, an organization to which she is now a proud member. Edna's contribution in this anthology, "Taino Woman-Child," is her memorial to the Taino Nation, the First Nation to discover Christopher Columbus anchored upon the shoreline of their island homeland.

Heather MacLeod: has lived in Yellowknife for the past several years. She was born in 1964 in Alberta, was raised throughout British Columbia and the Yukon and is of Cree and Scottish descent. She has left Yellowknife for the past few winters as she is working towards a degree in Creative Writing from the University of Victoria. Heather writes short stories, plays, articles and poetry. She is currently working on a book of poetry.

Victoria Lena Manyarrows: is Native/Mestiza (Eastern Cherokee) and 37 years old. She was raised alongside reservations and within mixed communities in North Dakota and Nebraska. As a young person, she spent a year in various foster homes. Since 1981, she has worked extensively with community arts and alcohol/substance abuse programs in the San Francisco Bay area. She has a Master's degree in Social Work. Her essays and poetry have been published in various Native and multicultural publications in the United States and Canada. As a writer, activist and artist, her goal is to use written and visual images to convey and promote a positive Native-based world view.

Lee Maracle: Born on the West Coast of British Columbia of Salish/Metis heritage, she is the mother of four and grandmother of two. She currently resides in Toronto where she was guest lecturer at the University of Toronto in the fall of 1993. Besides writing, she makes her living as an Empowerment and Cultural Reclamation counsellor. She is author of two novels, *Sundogs* and *Ravensong*, two non-fiction works, *Bobbi Lee* and *I am Woman*, and *Sojourner's Truth* a collection of short stories. She has published in over a dozen anthologies as well as numerous journals and magazines.

Janet McCloud: (Indian name YET SI BLUE) is a member of Tulalip Tribes, western Washington. She was born March 30, 1934. She was married to Don McCloud until his death April 10, 1985. She is the mother of eight—six daughters, two sons, and at this time about 30 grand - and great grand-children (five are adopted). She has been active for over 30 years in various struggles as a grassroots organizer. She is now semi-retired, but still lectures nationally and internationally. She works mostly at home on youth issues and training younger Native women.

Carol McFadden: is Tsimshian, Coast Salish and Irish. She was born in 1961 and survived her childhood in white foster homes. She presently resides in Victoria, B.C. with her four-year-old son who fills her heart. She is happy and proud to be who she is - NATIVE.

Scott Kayla Morrison: A Choctaw author, she currently organizes Indian communities for a national environmental group, Jobs and the Environment Campaign, based in Boston. Her publications include, *The Luddington Papers* and *The Lawsuit*. She is a newspaper social correspondent for News from Indian Country of Hayward, Wisconsin and the The Circle of Minneapolis. "Chances With Wolves" is Morrison's regular column in the environmental newsletter *Communities of Resistance*. She is also editing *A Handful of Dirt*, an anthology of Native writers to fund Native environmental organizing.

Marcie Rendon: White Earth Anishinabe, Mother and writer.

Doris Seale: Father, Santee and Cree; Mother, French and English. Current occupation, children's librarian. Her publications include *Books Without Bias: Through Indian Eyes*, with Beverly Slapin, *Blood Salt*. She is a contributor to *Fireweed* and *A Gathering of Spirit*, "1492-1992, and American Indian Perspective" in *The Multi-Colored Mirror*. Forthcoming: "Willy Horse's Child" in *Re-Inventing the Enemy's Language*. Her work in progress is *The People With Six Fingers*, a novel.

Vickie Sears: is a Cherokee/Spanish/English writer and therapist living in Seattle, Washington. She is also a teacher of cross-cultural therapy. She has published articles on therapeutic topics and been widely anthologized in books of poetry and short stories. She has published her own collection of short stories entitled *Simple Songs*.

Jaune Quick-to-See Smith: is an enrolled member of the Flathead Tribe in Western Montana. She is a painter who exhibits internationally. She is also an activist/spokesperson for contemporary Native American artists. She founded two cooperatives: the Coup Marks on the Flathead Reserve and the Grey Canyon Artists in Albuquerque. She curated the touring exhibit of *Our Land Our Selves: Contemporary Native American Landscape* for SUNY, Albany with 30 artists, and organized and curated the touring exhibit of *The Submuloc Show or the Columbus Wohs* with 35 Native Americans. She has just completed curating and writing the catalog for the exhibit, *We the Human Beings* for Wooster College, Ohio which features the works of 27 Native American contemporary artists.

Nicole Tanguay: Born of Ojibway and French Canadian parents, she grew up in foster homes and has been working for the equality of all women, especially First Nations women, and for the freedom of all Indigenous people the world over.

Lenore Keeshig-Tobias: is an award-winning author and story-teller. She was born on the Neyaashiinigmiing (Cape Croker) reserve in Ontario, where she now lives. She has three grown daughters, a grand-son, and a young daughter and son. As a culture worker, she has worked on anti-racist issues through the arts, particularly on the issue of cultural appropriation. She shares the 1993 Living the Dream Award, with her daughter, Polly, for their book *Bird Talk* . Lenore is presently employed as anti-racism coordinator for the Saugeen Ojibway First Nations.

Laura Tohe: is from the Tsenahabinii clan and born for the Tohdichinii clan. From her mothers she learned that when we create, we never do it alone; there is always some creative force helping us, guiding us, because we humans are not perfect. She calls shikeyah, home, what is referred to as the Navajo reservation. In her writing place/home is an important ingredient: "I couldn't write if I didn't have a sense of place where I can imagine poems and stories happening." Laura has two children.

Debra Haaland Toya: is an enrolled member of the Pueblo of Laguna in New Mexico and was born in Winslow, Arizona in 1960. Her ancestry is that of Norwegian and Laguna and Jemez Pueblo. Winslow was her birthplace because her Indian grand-parents lived there, working on the Santa Fe Railroad for 45 years. Her Norwegian father was in the U.S. Marine Corps; therefore, her family travelled extensively across the U.S. for most of her childhood. When her father retired in Albuquerque, they stayed for the closeness to their ancestral lands at Laguna Pueblo. She is currently obtaining a B.A. in English at the University of New Mexico. She has been published in *New Mexico Magazine, Wicazo Sa Review* and in the forthcoming book *Reinventing the Enemy's Language*. She cooks, enjoys creating art with cake and icing, and performs ceremonial dances at least five times per year.

Haunani-Kay Trask: is author of *From a Native Daughter: Colonialism and Sovereignty in Hawai'i*, a collection of political essays; and *Light in the Crevice Never Seen*, a book of poetry. She teaches in the Hawaiian Studies Center at the University of Hawai'i.

Gail Tremblay: is Onondaga/Mic Mac and was born in Buffalo, New York. She currently teaches at the Evergreen State College in Olympia, Washington, and is a working artist and poet. Her last book of poems *Indian Singing in 20th Century America* was published by Calynx Press.

CREDITS

The anthologizer and the publisher would like to thank the following for their kind permission to reprint copyright material in this book:

POETRY

Chrystos, "The Real Indian Leans Against" from *MS*, October, 1992. Reprinted with permission of the author.
Fife, Connie "Resistance" and "Stones Memory" from *Beneath the Naked Sun*, Sister Vision Press, 1992. Reprinted with permission of the publisher.
Blaeser, Kimberly "Living History" from *Loonfeather*, Fall/Winter 1991, Vol.12, No.2. Reprinted with permission of the author.
Tanguay, Nicole "Halfbreed" from *Fireweed*, Weird Writing Issue, No. 31, Fall 1990. Reprinted with permission of the author.
Caldwell, Kim "Bad Taste in My Mouth" from *Perpetua, the Magazine*, Vol.1, Issue IV, April 1993. Reprinted with permission of the author.
Keeshig-Tobias, Lenore "O Canada (bear V)" from *Toronto Star*, July 1990. Reprinted with permission of the author.
Damm, Kateri "To You Who Would Wage War Against Me" from *My Heart is a Stray Bullet*, Kegedonce Press, 1993. Reprinted with permission of the author.
Hogan, Linda "It Must Be" from *Savings*, Coffee House Press, 1988. Reprinted with permission of the author.
Armstrong, Jeannette "Death Mummer" and "First People" from *Breathtracks*, Theytus and Williams-Wallace, 1991. Reprinted with permission of the publishers.
Harjo, Joy "For Anna Mae Pictou Aquash" and "The Real Revolution is Love" from *In Mad Love and War*, copyright 1990 by Joy Harjo, Wesleyan University Press. Reprinted with permission of the publisher University Press of New England.
Sears, Vickie "Grandmother" from *Gathering Ground*, Seal Press, 1984 and "Old Ways Keeper" from *Calyx*, Vol.8, No.2, 1984. Reprinted with permission of the author.

Bell, Kathryn "Ester" from *The Phoenix-Oklahoma Poets*, North-eastern State University, Fall 1988. Reprinted with permission of the author and "Cordell, OK, 1950" from *Piecework*, Fall, 1986. Reprinted with permission of the author.

Dumont, Marilyn "Squaw Poems" and "Helen Betty Osborne" from *The Road Home*, Reidmore Books, 1992. Reprinted with permission of the author.

Manyarrows, Victoria-Lena "Braiding/Ribbons of Revolution" from *Voices of Identity, Rage and Deliverance: An Anthology of Writings by People of Mixed Descent*, No Press, 1992. Reprinted with permission of the author.

Cuthand, Elizabeth "The Anglais, They Say" from *Voices in the Waterfall*, Lazara Press, 1987. Reprinted with permission of the author.

Marcie Rendon, "This Woman That I Am Becoming. . ." from *A Gathering of Spirit*, Firebrand Books, 1984. Reprinted with permission of the author.

FICTION

Maracle, Lee "The Laundry Basket" from *Voices: Being Native in Canada*, University of Saskatchewan Press, 1992. Reprinted with permission of the publisher.

Brant, Beth "This Is History - for Donna Goldleaf" from *Food and Spirits*, Press Gang, 1991. Reprinted with permission from the author and publisher, Firebrand Books.

Bear, Shirley "Diamonds of the Forest" from *Fireweed*, No.34, Fall, 1991. Reprinted with permission of the author.

ARTICLES

Awiakta, Marilou "Cherokee Eden" from *Selu: Seeking the Corn-Mother's Wisdom*, Fulcrum, 1993. Reprinted with permission from the author.

Beaver, Susan "Gays and Lesbians of the First Nations" from *Piece of my Heart*, Sister Vision Press, 1992. Reprinted with permission of the author.

SISTER VISION
Black Women and Women of Colour Press
was founded by Women of Colour in 1985. Sister Visions mandate and priority is publishing books by Black women, First Nations women, Asian women and women of mixed racial heritage.

The vision of Sister Vision Press came out of a need for autonomy, a need to determine the context and style of the work, words and images that are produced about us.

Our list features ground-breaking and provocative fiction, poetry, anthologies, oral history, theoretical writing and books for young adults and children.

A free catalogue of our books is available from Sister Vision Press, P.O. box 217, Station E, Toronto, Ontario, Canada, M6H 4E2, Phone (416) 533-2184.